"In my teens and twenties, I fought the assumption that you could not do various things like represent your community or stand for parliament, because you were too young. Now that I have started my 'second-half', I am becoming just as militant in fighting assumptions that you are now too old to do various things or start an entirely new career. Julie Perigo has produced a stimulating and practical 'how to' guide for making the most of increased life expectancy.

For those of us who want to live every day of our lives, *Winners in the Second Half* should be required reading. Not just the case for *carpe diem* but also for *carpe vitam!*"
Professor David Grayson
Director of The Doughty Centre for Corporate Responsibility, Cranfield School of Management and Author of *Everybody's Business* and *Corporate Social Opportunity*.

"Julie Perigo writes about one of the most topical and controversial issues of our day, both for senior individuals and the global economies in which we live: that of Extended Careers. What will they look like? How can the Second Half of our lives be even more successful, meaningful and *significant* than the First? Through vibrant examples drawn from her years in global executive search & from recent interviews, and through the self-audits for readers in each chapter she opens up new and aspirational options for anyone in later-career contemplating 'What's next?'"
Sue Cheshire
Co Founder and CEO of The Global Leaders Academy, Co Founder of The Academy for Chief Executives and contributor to International publication *Leadership is Global*

"This is a must-read for all executives in or approaching their own Second Halves. It provides a valuable checklist for those who want to confirm they are on the right track – and practical tools and straightforward advice for all of us who want to super-charge our skills and experience in later-career. Highly readable, candid and thought provoking at a number of levels."
David Nosal
Chairman & CEO, Nosal Partners LLC

"Julie Perigo illuminates the 'later-career' phase with good clear analysis and marvellous stories. She is also very good on the practical connection between individual career and creative leadership in general. A first rate read."
Alistair Mant
International authority on leadership development and executive talent identification; author of *The Leaders We Deserve* and the best-seller *Intelligent Leadership*.

Winners in the Second Half

A Guide for Executives at the Top of their Game

Julie Perigo

JOSSEY-BASS
A Wiley Imprint
www.josseybass.com

Other Wiley Editorial Offices

John Wiley & Sons Inc., 111 River Street, Hoboken, NJ 07030, USA

Jossey-Bass, 989 Market Street, San Francisco, CA 94103-1741, USA

Wiley-VCH Verlag GmbH, Boschstr. 12, D-69469 Weinheim, Germany

John Wiley & Sons Australia Ltd, 42 McDougall Street, Milton, Queensland 4064, Australia

John Wiley & Sons (Asia) Pte Ltd, 2 Clementi Loop #02-01, Jin Xing Distripark, Singapore 129809

John Wiley & Sons Canada Ltd, 6045 Freemont Blvd, Mississauga, ONT, L5R 4J3, Canada

Wiley also publishes its books in a variety of electronic formats. Some content that appears in print
may not be available in electronic books.

Library of Congress Cataloging-in-Publication Data

Perigo, Julie.
    Winners in the second half : a guide for executives at the top of their game / Julie Perigo.
        p.   cm.
    Includes bibliographical references and index.
    ISBN 978-0-470-72537-5 (cloth : alk. paper)   1. Executives.   2. Career development.   I. Title.
    HD38.2.P466 2008
    658.4′09—dc22

                                                                                                2008015118

British Library Cataloguing in Publication Data

A catalogue record for this book is available from the British Library

ISBN 978-0-470-72537-5

Typeset in 11/15 pt Goudy by SNP Best-set Typesetter Ltd., Hong Kong
Printed and bound in Great Britain by TJ International Ltd, Padstow, Cornwall, UK

To my parents on their 60th anniversary, and to my husband on our 10th.
Well done!

Contents

Preface

The idea for this book was first prompted by my experiences when I was still a Partner in the world of Executive Search. I was finding more and more high-level executives in their 50s and 60s coming to me for advice and to be a sounding board for them regarding how they should approach their later-career period. I came to realise that there was not very much literature, or any other practical assistance, available to them.

Most books aimed at people in that age group seem to concentrate specifically on retirement, and on the financial aspects related to it rather than what they really wanted to talk about, which was: *'What shall I do next?'* And although the media is gradually taking notice of the issues around Extended Careers, the tendency is still to concentrate on blue-collar workers, and a one-size-fits-all approach.

It seems in many ways as if the senior managers, executives and public and private sector leaders, and their needs and desires concerning their Second Half (i.e. the years beyond 50), are being ignored. As if, simply by their likelihood of having more superannuation and savings than the average worker, they will somehow sail through the experience without the emotional, psychological, practical and spiritual anxieties that others go through.

My experience leads me to believe that quite the opposite is true. The experiences, transitions and decisions involved in working out what one's later-career is all about are often *harder* the higher up the corporate ladder you go.

That realisation led me to found Re-Inventors several years ago, an executive development and business strategy consultancy specialising in later-career policy. Since then our clients have been both large and smaller

organisations, concerned with how to cope with the ramifications of demographic change. We have provided assistance to them on, among other
related matters, knowledge management and the performance support and
retention of their older leaders. Through those organisations we have worked
closely with their senior individuals and, as a consequence, have developed
much of the material and case studies in this book.

I am also moved to write this because I believe that Extended Careers
must be part of the whole Sustainability agenda. Governments need us to
have these Extended Careers, individuals want to have them – but organisations still generally do not know how to provide and support them.

Through 'Winners in the Second Half', and through my executive developing and consulting work, my aim is twofold: to help senior individuals
play the best game possible in their Second Half and then in turn, as leaders,
go on to create new precedents and role models for the broader socio-
economic community.

The upbeat sporting metaphor of the Second Half, and its extension
throughout the book, seemed to me to be particularly apposite for framing
the positive nature of this topic. Too many real 'players', in every sense of
the word, who have been extraordinarily successful in their own First Half,
allow themselves to be taken in by an outdated fear that life and career fall
into a big black hole after the age of 50. Instead of seeing the opportunities
and growth available in later-career and beyond, they see only exclusion
and decline.

In this book my intention is to show that today's transition into the
Second Half is not about the transition into retirement, but about a transition which is reinvention. Most fundamentally it is an invitation to give
oneself permission to return to one's authentic self, to re-explore and live
out one's real interests – and let go of the ladder, which has been one of the
greatest inhibitors to later-career fulfilment since the 1950s.

Time and again in my interviews and research I have heard senior individuals voice their own belief that they are just hitting their stride in their
50s. It's not surprising they feel this way. It is the time in adult development
when they are starting to move into a phase of Generativity. The attributes
associated with it are almost exactly synonymous with what Jim Collins calls
'Level 5 leadership', the highest level in the hierarchy of executive capabilities that he identified.

The biggest fear at the top of the ladder is, *'Where do I go to from Success?'*
The biggest thrill is knowing that beyond it can be Significance. My intention is to offer a framework, and a motivation, to achieve that. So within
the book I have divided each of the following seven chapters into two distinct sections.

The first section offers real-life case studies to illustrate key Second Half
challenges including career plateaus, relationships, ageism, planning for the
future, leaving a worthwhile legacy and the meaning of 'enough'. Through
a variety of typologies and archetypes, opportunity is created for reflection
on the variety of approaches and responses available – and their varying
degrees of efficacy.

In each second section ('Developing the Gameplan') there are highly
practical exercises to allow readers to go more deeply into their own personal
situations and needs, and come up with solid options and guiding
principles.

I hope this format will prove particularly valuable, as one of the most
consistent responses I encounter in my work is, *'I just never have time to think
about this sort of stuff. And I don't have the frameworks.'*

To gain maximum benefit from the second section I strongly recommend
that readers go through it twice over. Once on your own for personal
insights, then over again with a significant other (or several) for an even
clearer, more enlightening, perspective.

So, let me wish that you find meaning, significance and pleasure in
reading this book – and that you find exactly the same in your own Second
Half!

Acknowledgements

Firstly let me acknowledge the role of Peter Trout. Without our chance conversation over Sunday lunch one day several years ago I may never have come up with the idea of this book or of my work today.

I would like to thank all the people in the USA, Australia, the UK, Asia and Europe who have given their time and insights to me in interviews and in research for this book. In particular: David Nosal, Mike Butcher, Lord Adair Turner, John McFarlane, Gavin Freeman, Steve Connard, Lance Moir, Dan Dumitrescu, Professor Louise Rolland, Clive Landa, Dr Geoffrey Thomas, Juliane Michaels, Kim Haywood-Matty, Gerhard Rumpff, Gareth Bennett, Bob Lumpkins, Eunice Azzani, John Forman, Robin Squire, Dan Veatch, Mark Henderson, Laura Mazur, Terry Seno, Mark Wooding, Shane Freeman, Sue Cheshire, Caspar Robinson, Wayne Achurch, Helen Woods, Stephen Boley, Jane Lorand, Michael Morgan, Roger West, Russell King, Ian Grant, Tess Finch-Lees, Michael McDermott, Olle and Nina Hammarstrom, Professor Philip Taylor, Laurel Ross, Liz Broderick, John Barraclough, John Wright, David Combie, Neil Watson and Richard Oldcorn.

My gratitude also goes to all the candidates and clients over the years who have provided me with such a wide and fascinating set of case studies, questions and input.

Dr Pat McCarthy at RMIT in Melbourne provided me with a wealth of support, research and feedback on the issues faced by individuals in later-career. Professor Sharon Moore in Sydney and Professor David Grayson, Director of the Doughty Centre for Corporate Responsibility at Cranfield, gave me very welcome encouragement as a first-time author. Along with my colleague Sharon Jackson at the Cambridge Gateway Academy, and founder of Carlton CSR, David also helped me articulate the importance of personal career Sustainability within the context of corporate, economic and global Sustainability.

My gratitude to Paul Porteous and Robbie McPherson. Their influence on the Sydney Leadership Programme at The Benevolent Society led me to give up a nice safe corporate job and have the courage to keep pushing my peanut forward. Similarly, the enthusiasm and camaraderie from Ed Williams, Kathryn Hodnett and Neil Wragg around the Winners in the Second Half Programme helped keep me focused on my mission.

I send my thanks also to Fred Kofman and the Partner group at Axialent who gave me the time to devote to this work.

My appreciation too to the team at John Wiley who all had great patience as I moved from Sydney to San Francisco to Stockholm and to Henley during the course of writing! Thanks especially to Francesca who commissioned the work, to Viv who helped me through the detail involved in getting the manuscript together, and also to Jo and Natalie. Maria Rados at Sapio AB in Stockholm was also a life-saver in helping me collate and print the final manuscript.

Last, but definitely not least, my love and thanks to those closest to me. To my dear husband who has so wholeheartedly encouraged me, and acted as my guinea pig for many of the exercises. And to my amazing parents, the ultimate examples of the benefits of a sea change. A more impressive team you could not wish to meet in their Second Half.

1

Winning in the Second Half
OR
Seize a new opportunity

'So what are you going to do when you grow up?'

Those of us born since World War II have something to look forward to which no other generations in the history of the world have ever had: exceptional longevity. Most of us currently in our 40s and 50s will live until we are around 100. With my genes and lifestyle my GP predicts I'll keep going until 102.

Whereas we can expect to live until around 100, our parents and grandparents had little expectation of living much beyond 60 or 65. There was no point in them bothering to try to map out and make sense of a time of life which simply wasn't going to exist for them.

Unconscious stereotyping

Throughout recorded history, only one in ten people could expect to live to 65. It is hardly surprising therefore that the psychology of our society has developed over many generations so that we have now unconsciously conditioned ourselves to believe that we work until our 60s . . . go into rapid decline . . . then die. This is despite the evidence of our own eyes and personal experiences these days.

As individuals, our mental models are built consciously and unconsciously upon role models, particularly those formed in childhood and youth. Our rational adult minds know full well that increased longevity nowadays has not just added years, but has added fitness, health and vigour to those years. Increasingly we see headlines on, '60 is the new 40'.

And yet our mental images and the self-limiting beliefs that arise from them, tend still to focus on the long outdated role models we bring from our earliest years: our grandparents and their peers. And these have transmuted to become the grey-headed, grey-attitude stereotypes we carry around in our heads, largely without realising.

That's why we still carry the recollection of how early retirement was the Holy Grail. Back in the 1960s and 1970s it was painted as the reward for a lifetime of hard work, coupled with the assumption that it would be all beer and skittles. The reality was more desperate than that. It had less to do with money earned and assets amassed, and far more to do with the opportunity to steal back a few short years of vitality beyond the confines of 'work' before one's likely death.

The prospect of early retirement today is markedly different. It is no longer about trying to fit everything in to a mere handful of years. It has far more to do with wondering what we will do *to fill up* the next 20, 30 or 40 years ahead. And there are just as many concerns about abundance of time as there used to be about its scarcity.

We know that subliminally. Indeed, today when most high-achieving 50-somethings are polled, their quizzical response tends to be, 'What, *me* retire?!?' The answer isn't just about money, or the ability to fund it (although of course with an increased number of years likely to be ahead that can be an issue). It has far more to do with the concerns of, *'What would I do? Who would I be? . . . because I've got an awful lot of years ahead!'*

I was moved to consider writing this book whilst I was still in the Executive Search (head-hunting) field. I began noticing that a very large number of my candidates and clients in their late 40s and 50s were getting themselves caught up in 'baggage' around the concept of an inevitable, impending retirement. In most cases I found they were looking at it along extremely traditional lines, as if it were an ON/OFF button. As if they only had a 'career' whilst working full-time and moving ever upwards on a promotion ladder – then suddenly had no 'career' any more if they moved diagonally, or in a new direction, or undertook anything which was not full-time, nor as well paid.

And I became acutely aware of how this ON/OFF button approach, and the gap between stereotypes and their own personal reality, affected their mood, behaviour, performance and whole life. The images it conjured up for them were not based on the reality of what they saw today and who they knew themselves to be in their 50s and into their 60s. The images came from much further back in their pasts, the stereotypes exacerbated by a fear of age discrimination.

It was fascinating to watch the variety of responses too: denial, bitterness, frustration, acceptance or, in surprisingly few cases, alacrity.

Harder for high flyers

The theory that I have developed, through my work and in the interviews for my research, is that it is generally far harder for leaders and topflight executives to go through this Second Half transition than it is for the average worker. The A-Type Achievers who come to identify themselves through their power, position and prestige paint themselves into a corner if they continue with the ON/OFF button attitude. It leaves no space for innovation and attitudinal change. It feeds the temptation to aim at continuing the same style of successes of the First Half of life: partly to stay squarely in their comfort zone, and partly through sheer fear of the unknown. What can they see as the alternatives? There are as yet so few role models for us to aspire to.

That's where the sporting analogies concerning Second Halves, like playing and winning, etc., start to come in useful. An executive at the top of their game is very much like an elite athlete. Success is wonderful and all-consuming, fuelled by passion and determination. The aim is to reach peak performance and the desire is to stay there as long as possible. Of course that cannot last forever. So what happens *beyond* the peak? How do elite athletes adapt to what comes after? What aspects can be shared, and what lessons can be learned in the broader context of work and life?

According to the ex-international sports stars and Olympians to whom I have spoken, their experience is that finding what's beyond can be even harder, psychologically, than the effort of getting to the peak itself.

There are a number of books aimed at higher income earners, which concentrate on the financial aspects of later-career and beyond. My concern with them is that they avoid the point of *what* you want to do and be at this largely unexplored stage of life – and therefore stay at the lowest levels of Maslow's hierarchy of needs.

Frankly I don't believe that is meaty enough for those of you who have been pushing your intellectual and innovational envelope for years. Besides, as executives you are likely to be in the top economic quartile concerning your assets and therefore beyond the Maslow's survival level of enough to live on (which of course many others are not).

Beyond that point the existential question is no longer, 'How much money will I have?', but 'What do I want the money in order to do and to be?' Whenever I've spoken to Financial Advisors about the subject, they have told me that the *doing* and to an even greater extent, the *being* are commonly very vague and unplanned areas in their clients' minds. They are brushed aside by motherhood statements like travelling or paying off the debts. They tell me that very often the ones who put least thought into 'what comes next?' are those with the most money.

Simply because we have money it does not mean that we can magically 'live happily ever after'. Similarly, just because as high-level managers we may have been supposed to have all the answers to corporate questions, by dint of the authority and titles we assumed, it does not mean we will automatically have all the answers to what comes after that. As Jane Fonda quipped recently, 'I'm over the hill – but nobody prepared me for what was going to be on the other side.'

Now that we have a good chance of being around until 100, we have literally *almost half a lifetime more* than previous generations did. Not only that but, in the corporate world, we are likely to have peaked earlier and have achieved what purports to be the pinnacle of success somewhere in our 40s, even 30s.

It brings us, inescapably, to confront the question, 'What is Success beyond Success?, What will "winning" look like in our Second Half?' Whatever you choose it to be, it is a new opportunity to be seized.

The current, typical focus for 'Success'
centres around our mid 30s to late 40s …

➡ 30 ⬅ 40 ⬆ 50 ➡ 60 ➡ 70

Yet in the 21st century we all need to plan for our **Extended Careers.**
We will have more time post 'Success' than preparing for it ….

Figure 1.1 Model for 21st century Extended Career

As all good leaders know, it is one thing to recognise an opportunity, but the magic of turning it into success comes through how we define it and how we frame the challenge in our mind in order to take best advantage of it.

Choosing the right words

There is enormous power in how we frame our thoughts. The very words we use, the metaphors and the mental images affect our understanding, our attitude and our behaviour. Take the positive impact of the metaphor of approaching the years over 50 as if it is one's Second Half.

Why 'Second Half'? As it is in our nature to err towards completion, we can hardly think of it without finishing the sentence . . . 'Second Half *of the Game*'. And wonderfully quotable individuals from Shakespeare to Quentin Crisp and Alexis de Tocqueville to Joseph Brodsky have all affirmed that 'Life is a Game'. It's a common way to describe life – and nearly always with positive connotations. It gives us a sense of 'all in it together', 'playing', 'winning', 'being part of the team'. Not necessarily easy – but always upbeat.

According to the research of Dr Patrick McCarthy at RMIT University, the years from 50 onwards are a time when we are likely to feel that we are losing control over our career and ambitions, and feeling forced to move outside the comfort zones we have painstakingly built up over decades. So framing our thoughts through a positive, hopeful, empowering metaphor is therefore extremely helpful in coping with that by recasting our conditioned, largely unconscious, attitudes towards what we do in our 50–100 period.

I ran the concept past an acquaintance in San Francisco. 'But what if someone's life hasn't been much of a game so far?' he countered. My reply to him was along the lines of, 'Well, why not consider turning it into one? The Second Half is as good a time as any to start. If not then, . . . when?'

Additionally, associated with the image of life as a game, is the concept of the successful person as a Player. It is becoming very popular to describe today's A-Type successful executives as 'players' too, which gives it an even stronger meaning.

It is a central image within the works of writers on leadership like Fred Kofman, who says: 'You must take unconditional responsibility; you need to see yourself as a "player", as a central character who has contributed to shaping the current situation – and who can thus affect its future. This is the opposite of seeing yourself as a "victim", subject to forces beyond your control. The Player is *in* the game and can affect the result. The Victim is *out* of the game and can only suffer the consequences of others' actions' (Kofman, 2006).

Focusing on the words themselves, compare the positive vibrancy of *winning, excitement, stamina, performance, goals, Player, energetic* connected with a sporting Second Half with any of the following:

• Never too old!
• Turning 50 or 60
• Becoming a senior citizen
• Retirement
• The Third Age
• Age Concern

What images came to mind for each word or phrase? How does your mind and body react to those images? How do you feel about identifying yourself with those words and images?

Unless I'm very much mistaken, the second set of words will be redolent of negative images for you. As you read them, your eyebrows are likely to have furrowed, you may notice an involuntary wry, even cynical smile rise to your lips. If you said them out loud the tone of your voice would probably strike others as disengaged at best, disapproving at worst.

There is nothing wrong with those words in themselves – but they have no attractive, inspiring connotations. They are not images that red-blooded individuals would actively aspire to. They are not . . . sexy!

As individuals, as couples, as families, as organisational cultures we all have particular words which jar on our ears, and which quite literally strike the wrong note. The words acquire 'baggage' and negative meanings and emotions become attached to them. When that happens, rightly or wrongly, they begin to influence the way we think about concepts to which they are attached.

From my MBA days, in our Marketing classes, I remember hearing how unsuspecting firms made horrendous mistakes by choosing words and names for their products which turned out to have dreadful, or risible, connotations in certain markets. They were perfectly good products, but the words used to create an image in the mind totally put off the buyers.

Words have absolutely the same effect in shaping how we look at concepts like age and later-career, in whether we view them and act on them happily, as an opportunity, or alternatively as a frustration or disappointment.

There is the salutary story of the Chevy Nova in South America. The company was apparently unaware that 'no va' means 'it won't go'. After the company figured out why it wasn't selling any cars, it renamed the car the Caribe in its Spanish markets.

When I was in China, as a young student, I was both fascinated and aghast to find a brand of ladies' sanitary napkins subtitled: 'Raise the Red Flag High!' And my Romanian brother-in-law always does a double-take when he sees the chain of women-only gyms in the USA called 'Curves'. It is the direct translation for 'Prostitutes' back home.

Most of those are simply attributable to bad translations. But there are also numerous examples of how, when we think we're speaking the same language, differing generational or national interpretations can leave others with a totally different understanding of what *we* believe the word or phrase to mean: for example, I can never seem to entice American dinner guests to try my mother's recipe for good old English Toad in the Hole or my father's favourite, Spotted Dick.

The Scandinavian vacuum manufacturer Electrolux, no doubt through its terribly talented, fluent English-speaking marketers still fell into the 'right word, wrong connotation' trap. 'Nothing sucks like an Electrolux' may be technically true . . . but sounds like a complete loser to North Americans and like a complete pervert to most English.

By the same token there are generational dissonances. When I hear that something is 'really bad', 'wicked!', or that someone is 'quite cool' about my proposal, I feel the need to work out the age of the speaker to make sure I interpret the message correctly.

And what about the gender-contextual words? There is nothing intrinsically wrong with the word 'girls'. It is a perfectly apt description of young females up to and around puberty. Seemingly many men consider it a cute compliment to call their mature women staff or family 'girls'. Yet an equal number of mature women, myself included, feel their hackles rise when addressed like that, perceiving within it an irritating superciliousness and patronisation.

Reframing our perceptions

In short, the words we use have tremendous impact on the way we perceive a message. They are central to the way we frame our opinion and understanding. Changing our words to describe something can radically change our attitudes towards it. Words can change an image: from good to bad, or bad to good. Certain words act as a taboo, ensuring we keep the associated theme veiled and thereby not discussable.

This has clearly happened about the subjects of later-career, ageing and retirement. As Ernest Hemingway remarked, 'Retirement is the ugliest word in the language'.

A huge range of benefits can be accrued through reframing and reconnecting the previously *separate* concepts of later-career and retirement. One's career and leadership engagement do not cease just because one is no longer necessarily working full-time, nor in high executive capacity. It is simply how one plays the Second Half.

There are many examples of reframing which can turn a taboo or uncomfortable subject into something totally affirmative. Until quite recently, 'bald' was one of those taboo words, relegating the topic of men with no or receding hair to the realms of comic turns and embarrassment. Yet, 'shaven head' and the sight of a Beckham-esque male have suddenly given the same look a very different standing in what we consider attractive, ugly or laughable.

In the same way, remember how condemnatory the word 'queer' was until it became replaced in our general parlance by 'gay & lesbian'. The descriptor 'queer' moved from being one that was in broadest common use, to one which now shows the speaker as having something significant against homosexuality.

Think also of the use of words like 'Negro' or 'Black', with the overtones of segregation and prejudice, which have gradually metamorphosed into the terms of respect of 'person of colour' and 'African American'.

And look at the power and optimism of the descriptor 'people living with AIDS' in contrast to 'AIDS victims'.

The metaphors and mental images of sport are central to recasting the attitudes we have about the years of 50 and beyond. Yes, it is about winning, AND it carries with it the Olympic ideal about playing simply for the love of the game. It is about performance and, quite literally, goals. It is about playing (as in 'fun') and about being a Player in all senses of the word.

Winning in the Second Half

I asked Tim, a Partner at KPMG in London, what images those words brought back for him:

> For me, I'm back in my first year at Secondary School. My first taste of external competition in a soccer game against another local boys' school, playing against people whom for once I didn't know. The First Half had been exhilarating, challenging. And it had been a bit of a blur too. A lot of running up and down the pitch, with not much strategy in mind, but a lot of loose energy.
>
> I hadn't known quite what to expect, and I was pretty much doing everything on instinct. Yes, we had been given some rudimentary tactics to try to employ – but it all seemed to move so fast that I remembered them only after I realized I'd done something different: passed to the wrong person, taken the ball up the wrong side or forgotten to mark my opponent in the chase for possession. But we were ahead by two goals when the Half-Time whistle blew.
>
> Half-Time was like being pulled back out of some dream. Our Soccer Coach, Mr Wright, cut through the buzz of 'activity' and brought us back to earth with three instructions: one was about marking, one was about pacing ourselves and the third, I distinctly remember was, 'Pass up to Mark. Let him shoot!' How sensible that all sounded. How calming.
>
> But when I heard the whistle and the words, 'We're about to start the Second Half' it felt different to before. We had, supposedly, learnt something about the opposition's tactics. We'd tested our own strengths and stamina. And yet we already had something to lose – our lead. Somehow it wasn't the same as going on the field at nil-all at the start of the game. Better? Worse? Just a bit different.
>
> I remember that sensation of stepping out there again. Heart in my mouth, excited. Keen as mustard to get right back out there and not make the silly mistakes of the First Half. And jolly well win!

My father and I were great fans of Welsh rugby and, back in the 1970s, when the Welsh team was in one of its cyclical heydays we used to go regularly to watch the internationals at Cardiff Arms Park or at Twickenham. But one of the best games I ever saw was on TV, when Wales were playing Scotland in 1971 away from home.

It had been a nail-biter right from the start. The lead had swung from one team to the other, and there was plenty of action in both halves. All the stars were on form. Then, right in the dying minutes of the game, when the score was 18–14 to Scotland, Gerald Davies the Welsh winger sneaked in a try – but the Scottish defence managed to keep him well away from the posts.

That took the score to 18–17. As the ball had to be placed on the right-hand side, the conversion looked almost impossible, particularly as Barry John, the usual Welsh kicker, had been concussed earlier in the match. I remember I could hardly bear to watch, as the suspense was so palpable. It was John Taylor who stepped up to take it and, although he was never a regular kicker for the side, managed to place it exquisitely between the posts the second before the final whistle blew. It neatly secured the Triple Crown and the Grand Slam for Wales. What a thriller.

And what was the point of that story? That in sport there is no 'value judgement' made about either half. The First Half of a match is not considered intrinsically better than the Second Half. The first and second halves of a race are also both equally important.

And to take it even a step further, the Second Half could be considered in certain ways *more* important. However good someone is in the First Half, however much of a lead they build up, they can only really count themselves a winner when the final whistle blows or they touch the finishing tape. And to get to that point it's all about performing in the here and now, living in the present – and not losing concentration by looking forward, backwards or sideways.

If anything, in sport, going in to the Second Half is often even more exciting – especially if the First Half has been dull and predictable. There is always the hope, by players and spectators alike, that it will ignite into something spectacular.

The Extended Career

Linked with reframing the Second Half of our 100 years in such a positive pro-active format, is that our understanding of what we mean by 'career' is sorely out of date. We need a new mindset about it, and one that is not cluttered up by traditional notions of age and retirement.

This should help put it in perspective: Do you know how the consensus on a specific retirement age originated? It was because when Bismarck introduced the Old Age Pension in Prussia in the late 1880s he is purported to have asked his civil servants, 'By which age are most of them dead?'

So the pensionable age was set at 70 (but shortly after lowered to 65), meaning that only approximately 2% of the population at the time were alive to take advantage of it. That 2% or so, because of the health conditions at the time, were generally assumed to be disabled and therefore incapable of work. So, general health conditions at that time and State Pensions together managed to set in concrete the view that life beyond 'pensionable age' is about inactivity and rapidly becoming geriatric.

Another conundrum is that in most systems the retirement age is set lower for women (60) than men (65), despite the fact that women generally live around five years longer than their male counterparts. It is somewhat bizarre that this assumption has remained largely unchallenged in the light of our enormous increases in longevity and fitness. Our Western societies have only recently begun to question it.

In a curious symmetry, the challenge comes from the same financial standpoint as Bismarck in the first place. Today's governments and Pensions Commissions find themselves with enormous gaps in pension provision. There are simply not enough funds available to continue to have the workforce retiring at 65 if they are going to need to draw pensions for another 30 rather than five years. So they are asking, 'By which age are they mostly still fit and healthy?' with the aim of moving the pensionable age later. If the fit and healthy workforce keeps working longer, there might just be enough to go round.

So suffice it to say that it's very likely that you *won't* retire, at least in the conventional sense of the word. You'll either be working for the money in order to fund lifestyle, children or just plain everyday expenses. Or you'll be engaged in some form of activity in order to keep yourself active, involved, fulfilled or even simply 'occupied'. The pressures (and supports) come from a variety of sources.

The reframing here is that the focus must move away from the ON/OFF button of traditional retirement to one's Extended Career. The heart of the matter is one's personal sustainability.

As Ken Dychtwald points out in both *The Age Wave* and *Age Power* (Dychtwald and Flower, 1990; Dychtwald, 2000), there are new trends

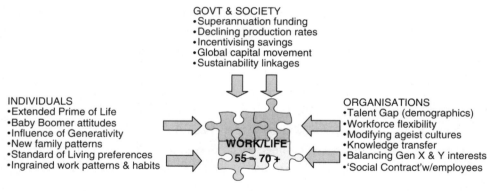

Figure 1.2 Influences on age and work

which see professionals go through two or three mini-retirements between their 50s and 70s. For some it is into serial project work, and this has fuelled the rise in interim management options. For others it is to part-time options, either by choice or simply availability. For still others it is the chance to explore running one's own business, or moving into a completely different style, or hierarchical level, of work. The latter options tend to be most appealing to high stress, burn-out victims.

What it shows is that the situation can be even more flexible when one is in the mid 50s–mid 70s period of worklife than it ever has been before. The corollary is that one's own flexibility towards it must be greater too in order to fully appreciate it.

So what is it you will actually be doing in your Second Half? More importantly, who will you be *being*?

A research survey I commissioned while at Highland Partners in 2004 (Highland Partners, 2004) asked a cross-section of management-level workers in their mid to late 50s, across three continents, what they saw themselves doing as purposeful activity beyond the age of 60. Nearly half of the respondents had either failed to come up with any ideas or hadn't stopped to consider the question at all before. Only just over 20% believed they had it all thought out and well planned.

At one level we could say, 'Perhaps it doesn't matter. Life will go on' and 'Things will sort themselves out'. Or, 'It can't be all that hard, everybody has to go through it'.

Yet I see a peculiar paradox here. What type of things do we most often try to put off thinking about and procrastinate upon? It's never the easy stuff, it's always the hard stuff. The great cop-out is to take the excuse of being

What do you see yourself doing in terms of 'purposeful activity' beyond age 60?

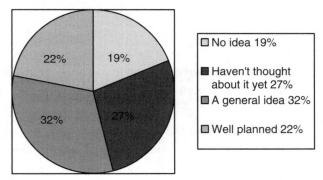

Figure 1.3 **Extended career planning**
Source: **Highland Partners Survey, 2004**

too busy to have the time to think. 'Normal' work is easy to focus on, as it's a known quantity. Later-career and beyond are unknown territory, and offer few viable role models yet.

There is a paradox too that these senior professionals, who are avoiding this question, are the very ones who would have had 12-month, three-year, five-year, even ten-year career plans from graduation onwards. I know, I've seen executives who in their 40s could enunciate those plans faultlessly and who were happy to spend quality time strategising those gameplans. And I've seen them ten years later in their 50s looking like rabbits in headlights when I asked what the next two years would hold, let alone the next ten.

Nor would they dare be so lax if setting strategy or product planning within their own field of business. In many ways products (or people) require least attention and maintenance when they are perceived to be at peak performance. Yet it is just as important to the sustainability of a business to work out what to do with a product which is moving towards the end of its cycle as it is in building it up in the first place. Handling the transition from cash cow to stable producer or fallen star can hit a bottom-line harder than a promising high-potential which never quite gets off the ground.

Part of my process has been to interview over 50 high-profile, very senior ex- and current executives and leaders in their fields, ranging from 48 to 78. But I've also talked in depth with a similar amount of professional people who haven't reached those dizzy heights – but would still fall into the Top 10% category.

In case it got your hackles up (as it did with some to whom I have mentioned my theme), the intention is certainly not to suggest that the

Chairman of a multinational or the founder of a household name business intrinsically knows any better about the uncharted territory of the Second Half than one of their Group GMs. The patterns that emerged did not support that theory at all. In fact, it is more a case of offering the comfort that the feelings of *uncertainty*, *unknown* and *unpreparedness* are shared across the board . . . except by those with the least imagination and capacity for self-awareness!

So, through this book I aim to point out some signposts, offer some real-life examples, suggest some frameworks and, most importantly, pose some probing questions to help you seize the opportunity to be a winner in the Second Half.

***

DEVELOPING THE GAMEPLAN:
Seize a new opportunity

Questions & activities to help you understand
and boost your attitude to the new period
of opportunity

1. Your life line

In the last 90 years longevity in the developed countries has increased by over 30 years. You could say we have each gained half a lifetime. These days in our 50s we are only at our Half-Time point.

So if you've picked this up, my guess is that you are likely to be around or beyond 50 yourself. Or you know someone close who is. Somewhere around that Half-Time point.

One of the CEOs I interviewed for this book, revealed to me what he thought was the most powerful, meaningful and memorable exercise he had ever been asked to do in his 30-odd years in senior management. He was asked to take a blank piece of paper and draw a horizontal line, putting his current age at the end.

_____ 47

Then he was asked to think of the three most formative experiences of his life to date, and mark on the line how old he was when each happened.

_____ 9 _____ 27 _____ 42 _____ 47

Next he was asked to extend the line to when he thought he would die, and mark on how old that would be . . .

To understand the impact that had on him, you really need to go through it yourself.

Another executive I had go through this commented:

> We had to draw this grid, mapping out our life and the significant points in it. The first aspect which made a big impression on me was that we had to plot our age by years, starting at birth and ending at death. What age should I put for that? I found myself instantly wondering if it would be the same age as my father, which of course brought him in as a reference point too, in my mind, for all that followed. I added a decade or so for myself on to the age he died.
>
> And the second major shock to the system was that it showed up how I had fewer years left than I had already lived. What a sobering thought. And how little time to go in what I thought of as my working life. What was I going to do with it? More than my father, I found myself thinking – and hoping.
>
> The exercise had a very profound effect on me, looking back.

So: take a blank piece of paper, or use the space below, and draw a horizontal line, putting your current age at the end.

Now think of the three most formative experiences of your life to date, and mark on the line how old you were when each happened.

Next, extend the line to when you think you will die, and mark there how old that would be . . .

> How do you feel about putting that down on paper?
> Does the time ahead feel like a blessing or a curse?

2. From the past to the future

A couple of years ago I saw the results of a survey of Europeans of both sexes and across a wide demographic. It had asked them when they predicted they would die . . . and when they would prefer to die. Most people thought they would die somewhere in their 80s, 90s or even beyond. But the most staggering aspect, as far as I was concerned, was that *the vast majority said they would prefer to die 10 years earlier than that!* What a waste of that opportunity . . . .

If you are approaching, or are already in the Second Half, it's likely that you have very vivid images for the years in the past. For your childhood years, your youth, teens, 20s and the years of your 30s and 40s.

> Are the years between around 55–75 as clear, looking forward, as the last 20 years of your life/career?
> When you were looking at what the future might hold when you were 30, what seemed to lie ahead?
> If you are somewhere in your 50s now, or nearing that point, how do the next 20 years look in comparison?
> What will be your three most formative experiences *of the future*?
> What will you be like?

I wonder what your responses to those questions about the Second Half look like for someone like you in the 21st century? Most people find themselves asking, what's life *supposed* to look like 0–50 vs. 50–100?

My bet is that it is not at all clear for you. Nor is it for most of us, if that is any comfort. Because no other generation has had the opportunity to live out this period before, there are precious few guidelines or role models for us to learn from. We all have the challenge now of trying to work these out as we go along.

3. Winning in the Second Half

'We're *starting the Second Half!*' Start by reading those words aloud.

> What images and feelings does that phrase conjure up for you?
> Excitement? Slight trepidation? A competitive urge? A sense of opportunity?

Now reread the story on page 9 about the vision which came to Tim's mind when he thought about an earlier type of sporting Second Half he had experienced.

What's your story of a memorable Second Half?

What game were you playing?

How did it feel?

Are there any lessons or messages in it for you around your own Second Half now?

Where are the parallels, where are the differences?

Look again at the account of the rugby Second Half on pages 9 and 10.

What famous Second Halves do you remember?

Were you playing in them, or watching them?

Do you think about one where the Second Half was a huge improvement on the First Half — or where it fizzled out?

What were the memorable aspects of it for you?

What sort of metaphors can you take from it as a way of looking at your own Second Half?

4. Sizing up and seizing

Positive, vibrant, high-impact words to associate with a great Second Half can include:

- Winning
- Excitement
- Stamina
- Performance
- Goals
- Player
- Energy, etc.

What words would you like to add to that list to keep as your own personal descriptors for your Second Half?

What words will best describe the way you want to live it out?

What sort of game do you see your life as?

Is it a sprint, a middle-distance race or a marathon?

Is it going to be the same game in the Second Half — or a new game?

Or possibly an updated set of rules?

Find time to discuss and share your answers with a colleague, friend or family member. Are they in a similar situation themselves, possibly in their Second Halves too? How can you support each other to gain maximum energy and centredness from the words and the images they evoke for you?

2

The game has changed
OR
Claim your Generativity

Over the course of our lifetime our attitude towards career and life changes, and so does the environment in which we operate. The 'game' we knew when we began our first job was not quite the same game we recognised when we first became Partner or reached the management ranks. The way we go about playing it changes too.

As we saw in the first chapter, the game we step into in later-career, in our Second Half, is different again. But are we seeing it with clear eyes and full awareness – or unconsciously hanging on to anachronistic assumptions?

For the first time in over a hundred years the linking of work involvement and of retirement to a specified age is being dismantled. The game, in a whole series of respects, is changing. There are a variety of forces upon us now to continue to participate in the workforce, some of them of our own creation, some of them economic or social pressures.

Government and society

Changing demographics and dramatic shortfalls in pension funding are fuelling a change of attitude by governments around the developed world, contrasting strongly with the 'retire early' trend which was prevalent when Baby Boomers were growing up.

Despite increasing cross-migration of younger workers from poorer communities into ageing developed populations, there is now an urgency for governments to raise the age of retirement or eschew the concept entirely.

This is because the sums needed to pay out 20 to 30 years of retirement pensions to the generation now approaching traditional retirement age are simply not there. In the 1950s there were eight 15–60 year olds for every person over 60, able to contribute to the production and taxes which would provide retirement pensions for the over 60s. This has now declined to 5 : 1. By 2050 it will be a mere 2 : 1. The pension gap is growing dangerously wider, as the ratio of pension-providers (producers) declines against the pension-receivers (retired).

The balance could be redressed somewhat if more people worked into their 60s and 70s. If that happened the total amount of pension funding needed would drop, as older workers either postponed taking pension or took part-pension and continued to work part-time. In addition, their production rates would add to the pension-funding coffers, improving the situation markedly. The alternative is the prospect of exorbitantly high taxes on younger workers, or vastly increased rates of federal borrowing, just to fund pensions for the next generations.

Across the world governments are becoming concerned at the low participation rates of the over 60s in the workforce. In 2000 the European Union set its Lisbon strategy, which aimed to increase productivity and economic stability through increasing the size and diversity of the labour group over the following 10 years. In addition to overall employment rates (70%), it set targets for gender equality participation rates (60% for women) and optimum participation rates for older workers (50%).

At present only the Scandinavian countries are approaching those targets and, as a consequence, their pension gap coverages are the healthiest in Europe. Germany, however, is estimated to need to borrow 3.5% compound to 2050 in order to fund its commitment gap. Austria too is in a similar position. The US position may require significant borrowing or tax rises, as sources suggest the existing fund could be exhausted by 2020.

If we look at the pension gaps in Southern Europe the gap widens dangerously too. And for the new Eastern European Member States of the EU, the gap is of disastrous proportions as they are also losing younger tax contributors to other Member States which increasingly undermines their *producer : recipient* pyramid.

If the older age group were only a small percentage of the potential workforce this would not be a burning issue. Unfortunately for the economy, those in the Second Half are becoming the majority. The Population Reference Bureau, a Washington, DC-based Not For Profit (NFP) demographic study group, predicts that by 2025 Americans over 65 will outnumber teenagers by 2:1. By the year 2050 they believe that as many as one in four Americans will be over 65, and many other demographers estimate that the median age in the USA will reach 50 around that same time.

Of all the stakeholders in the ageing workforce issue (government/society, organisations and individuals), it is the governments which therefore have the greatest axe to grind and thus the greatest responsibility to incentivise all sectors of business to retain, attract and develop the 50s, 60s and beyond in economic productivity.

Yet is this too much to hope for in democracies in which parties can expect an average of only four to eight years in government at best? Contentious policies such as incentivising the continuing development of later-career workers may be perceived as running the risk of losing votes among younger constituents, so only governments with bold social and economic policies will dare take the risk. As big business values its freedom and is usually antagonistic to anything resembling quotas or tokenism, governmental economic incentives will have to be demonstrably advantageous to change ingrained behaviours and expectations.

In spite of this, I still feel that it is the responsibility of any government which espouses long-term sustainability to begin the process of re-education about later-career work participation, supported by tax breaks and concerted incentivisation policy. If it does not take up a leading, influencing and even mandating role, businesses – in both private and public sectors – are likely to continue to be so Quarterly-focused that they will be blind to the bigger picture of impending talent shortage. They will continue to feel able to ignore the catastrophic effect that pension funding and low work participation rates will eventually have on the economy as a whole, in which they function.

Organisations

The figures mentioned above have been in the public domain for a couple of decades now. However the lag effect, due to our largely unconscious conditionings, means that as individuals, and especially as organisational workplace cultures, we are generally still living to yesterday's rules about work and age.

Baby Boomers (and probably most readers) were born in the post-war period in which there was a strikingly increasing birth rate, a rapidly decreasing infant mortality rate and therefore what appeared to be a never-ending supply of young people joining the working ranks. Our role models have been bosses and peers who have until now found it convenient to get rid of 'old codgers' so that the large volume of 'young turks' wouldn't feel bottle-necked and unable to gain their own rewards of power.

The 'bottle-necking' argument is still one I hear propounded by executives in their 50s and their organisations. It is a complex problem because, although the numbers are no longer there to support the argument across the board, it can still affect younger ambitious achievers if the senior players look as if they will be in the same roles for years to come. It can have a big impact on their morale, and therefore retention rates. As Shane Freeman, the GM of People Capital at ANZ Bank in Australia, and Dr Pat McCarthy of RMIT University propose, the answer is for organisations to become more innovative in how they continually refresh performance motivation by rotating certain responsibilities and setting new challenges so as to avoid stagnation and the image of 'bottle-necking'.

At the same time, in many high-profile environments the situation is quite the reverse. The problem there is a growing talent and leadership shortage, not bottle-necking. NASA, for example, estimates that 45% of its senior and middle management are eligible for retirement. That figure will rise to nearly 70% in two years' time. (See Broad, 2008.)

The teaching profession worldwide is facing severe shortages too. As a Euridyce Report (the information network on education in Europe) from 2002 notes, on average – across Europe – the bulk of teachers are in the 45+ age group and the industry norm is to take early retirement (Euridyce Report, 2002). The numbers coming into the profession are dropping well below replacement level, compounded by the fact that there is an increasing trend for younger teachers to leave the profession within three to five years of starting out in practice.

So the situation is more complex than it may at first seem. The solution for organisations is not as simple as to say 'keep the current leaders in the top leadership roles longer'. Although the numbers are no longer there to support an argument that older leaders should continue to step aside indefinitely for younger players, there is still the structural imperative for the momentum of succession-timing to be maintained. This is an issue we will come back to in Chapter 6.

Sadly, my experience to date is that organisations are the least likely of the three stakeholders to recognise or choose to do anything about the impending labour shortages and cultural impacts.

Fortunately, however, there is a growing band of organisations, particularly in the public and NFP sectors, and among the members of groups such as the UK's Business in the Community, which are actively seeking ways to retain, harness and extend the opportunities for older workers.

Interestingly, Board Directorships seem to be the one area which is benefiting from more progressive attitudes towards Extended Careers. According to my colleagues in the Search world, such as David Nosal (of Nosal Partners), the retirement ages for Directorships on Boards have been gradually pushing upwards from 68–70 to 72 or 75 in a number of cases. In his opinion the fundamental reason appears to be that these self-regulating groups have recognised that they do not wish to miss out on the skills and expertise of high-level individuals who are still fully fit and now more personally self-assured, better focused and more objective than they have ever been in their lives.

In general, however, regarding the executive management and leadership functions, the more usual response is, 'What's in it for us? They will only stay on for another few years anyway'. This response somewhat illogically ignores the fact that most of its younger workers will also leave within a few years too, yet they will probably have spent over ten times more money on developing and supporting them.

On the macro level this attitude ignores any responsibilities within the broader economic environment in which the business operates. An investment in assisting Extended Careers as a concept now is an investment in sustainability. Without it, all businesses will eventually feel the repercussions as taxes have to be raised to support the pension burden – which will no doubt be levied on corporations as well as individuals.

However, until later-career incentivisation and innovative methods for increasing participation rates are recognised as part of overall sustainability strategy, the short-sighted 'Quarterly Results' mindset is still likely to take precedence.

Individuals

So, while governments and organisations are still failing to actively get to grips with the issue, for better or worse, the responsibility for responding to the changed game then falls squarely on the individual. It falls most particularly on the leadership group as individuals in transforming their own attitudes, responses and behaviours. When those aspects change and reach critical mass, there is enormous scope for them to become champions and proselytisers within their sphere of influence, and change the situation for the better. We will continue to explore what this can mean in Chapter 7.

The key challenge to making Extended Careers viable at the knowledge worker and leadership level is maintaining peak engagement. It is about how to find Success beyond Success. Or, as I prefer, *Significance beyond Success*. And not just for the pleasure and good of the individual, but for the economic benefit of all. It is an archetypal Triple Bottom Line issue: affecting People, Planet and Profitability. It throws out the challenge to see how work, and our attitudes towards it, can be innovatively and profitably reworked to gain maximum benefit all round from Extended Careers.

As David Grayson, Director of The Doughty Centre for Corporate Responsibility at Cranfield University explains it,

> Encouraging Extended Careers is an integral part of being a responsible organisation and encouraging sustainability. First, because responsible organisations treat their employees well and look after them at all stages of their increasingly extended careers, so as to optimise their contributions and possibilities. Secondly, because sustainable development is about meeting the needs of today without compromising the possibilities for future generations – and that includes, above all, people themselves. Finally, there is plenty of anecdotal evidence that in later life, many of us get a greater sense of stewardship and understanding that we are only leaseholders of the earth's resources – with full repair and maintenance responsibilities, as a former British Prime Minister once said. That means that more of us want to play our part in leaving the world a better and more sustainable place.

Letting go of the ladder – and when is enough 'enough'?

Changing situations need changing responses. A major one is shifting how we look at the later stages of our career. Those in and around the Second

Half have been brought up with the view of their career as a ladder. This is strictly a 20th century invention, and one that is losing lustre for the Generations X & Y. The vogue for these younger generations is breadth and pragmatism, which steer their careers towards an increasing variety of experience and future options, as opposed to greater specialisation and thereby more closely proscribed choices. Prior to the 20th century, or certainly pre-World War I, the ladder of title and hierarchy was not as important as attaining the peak of one's profession in terms of mastery and 'a job well done'.

The concept of the career as a ladder has one blindingly obvious flaw for developed societies with an intention to keep a high participation rate among older managers. It is the question, 'Where do I go beyond the ladder?'

The top of the ladder, in executive terms, generally coincides with the final stage of one's work – with the next stage being a move into retirement. The flaw has become even more exposed because, for the last 25 years or so, the trend has been to reach the top of the ladder earlier, in one's 40s (see Figure 1.1). With another 50 years of life, and probably over 50% of that time likely to be in paid and active work, the obvious dilemma arises. 'So what will I do next?'

Closely linked to the ladder model is the contrast between *more* and *enough*. The whole image of a ladder implies the quest for 'more', and most Second-Halfers will have been brought up in a post-war era of 'striving for betterment', a 1960s fascination for increasing one's standard of living and a 1980s influence of Gordon Gekko's 'greed is good!' slogan.

So it can be a big jolt to the system to come to the point at which one's income ceases to be on the upward trajectory. It may stay the same, it may be less, but there will come a time when most people have to accept it will never be 'more' again.

It is worth remembering, however, that it is also at this point that there are likely to be *more* of a number of other very valuable things coming on to the scene – perhaps the most important being time!

And this is where the question of *enough* comes to the fore. Almost invariably when I ask, 'What is enough?', people's minds go directly to money. The majority of books on later-career and beyond concentrate on the financial aspects of 'enough'.

It is a very important aspect, of course. It was the question that Professor Shoshanna Zuboff said she always used to ask very early on in the Harvard Odyssey programme for later-career leaders, as it revealed so much about a person. A degree of financial independence allows the freedom to pursue all sorts of other self-realisation. But too much emphasis placed on it actually inhibits the likelihood of personal growth and fulfilment. Many of Professor Zuboff's students wrestled, metaphorically, with whether $10 million or $15 million would be 'enough'. Some readers of this book may worry about similar amounts and, even if not those amounts, will be in or above mid-management ranks and therefore earning, or have earned, well over the national average wage. So the question touches on far more profound values and needs than survival in Maslow's hierarchy of needs.

We have both financial and emotional needs, so we are selling ourselves short if we focus purely on money. Or purely on ourselves.

There is a lovely word in Swedish: 'lagom', which means 'just enough'. It comes from the days of the Vikings, when the community gathered to drink from the same bowl. It was understood that each person would drink 'laget om' – not too little to slake his own thirst, but not too much or it would deprive others of their fair share. The spirit of it is a sensible and respectful thoughtfulness, honouring one's own needs but having the sensitivity to gauge others' requirements too.

Generativity: the new definition of success

Following on from that, it seems a good point at which to introduce the concept of Generativity. As an idea and as a style of leadership to embody, it offers exceptional empowerment to us as individuals and undeniable value to our workplaces and society as a whole. I cannot understand why more people don't seem to be aware of it as a leadership concept, nor proselytise about it as a benefit inherently connected with Extended Careers and later-career leadership.

There are a variety of ways I have heard Generativity characterised:

- Capacity to give of oneself.
- Easing of ego.
- Care for the next generation.
- Interest in shaping a genuine legacy.

- Increase in desire for community and affiliation.
- Empathetic leadership.
- Community building.

I have heard its ethos and practice voiced over and over again in the interviews I have conducted with leaders in the later part of their careers. Yet, strangely, the model of Generativity was rarely named or acknowledged among these senior business people as a force for impactful leadership.

The term comes from the work of the psychologist Erik Erikson, known often as the father of adult development. In 1950 he first published *Childhood and Society*, in which he outlined his theory of human development as a series of eight stages (Erikson, 1993, new edition). It was the first time developmental psychology had focused beyond childhood and youth. Generativity was the term he coined to describe the concern with how to pass on to future generations what one has learnt in life. That and ego integrity, the achievement of a sense of personal wholeness and centredness, appear in his work as the defining attributes of Adulthood and Maturity.

Prior to that little attention had been paid to how one develops beyond adolescence. It was assumed that humans did not develop significantly in their attitudes and behaviours after the age of seven, as in the Jesuitical argument ('Give me the boy until the age of seven, and I will give you the man'). Or possibly not after puberty, because it was assumed to be the last point when large-scale hormonal changes were likely to affect one's physiological maturity. In the time of Erikson's own teacher, Sigmund Freud, 50 was considered very old, not the start of a Second Half likely to last to a completion at 100. In contrast to his pupil Erikson, Freud himself professed no interest in patients beyond that age, believing them incapable of noteworthy change in adulthood.

Even current authorities like Roger Gould (see, for example, Gould, 1979), Daniel Levinson (see, for example, Levinson, 1986) and Gail Sheehy began by concentrating on the under-65s, although the last has revised her original 'Passages' which stopped at 55 in the 1970s into a series stretching towards the age of 100. She now agrees that there's a revolution in our life-cycle and says, 'The fact that we are taking much longer to grow up and much longer to grow old shifts all the stages of adult life ahead by about 10 years. 50 is what 40 used to be. 60 is what 50 used to be. We now have, not

LIFE CHALLENGE / QUALITY	STAGE
Identity Establishment of oneself as a functioning individual. The start of I-awareness regarding values, tastes, opinions, etc.	Teens
Intimacy Development of self in relationship and mutual interdependence with others. The start of We-awareness regarding partner, friends, colleagues, etc.	20s
Career/Life Consolidation Finding and building one's social identity in the world. Continuing development of We-awareness as family, work and friendship groups	30s–40s+
Generativity Assuming wider focus to one's own life, and others, through development of selflessness and empathy. Increasing I- AND We-awareness to encompass broader community and related issues	50s–70s+
Integrity Acceptance of self, others and existence integrating I-and We-awareness and life experiences	70s–80s+

Figure 2.1 Generativity: stages of adult development

one, but several adult lives to be prepared for and mapped out' (Sheehy, 1999).

The way I generally present the developmental phases to the companies for which I consult, and to those who attend our later-career programmes (see www.CGAcademy.org), combines the original work of Erikson and the current research of George Vaillant.

If we look at life as divided into stages, at each one we encounter specific challenges related to our likely circumstances which call out new responses. Whilst childhood development can be linked quite exactly with age in months or years due to physical brain/body growth, the 'stages' for adults are clearly much less precise. And, just as some younger people stay stuck at a particular point of emotional development and fail to mature with the same interpersonal skills or inner awareness of their peers, it may well be that certain adults never move *into* the career consolidation phase, and others never move *beyond* it.

It would be my assumption though that those choosing, or perceived as having, a leadership role would move into each phase quite normally and respond to its 'challenge' extremely well. Some psychologists describe it as mastering a task. Personally I believe it is easiest to view it as embodying a response which one has *chosen*. This then becomes a mindset which creates a motivation which sets one's attitudes and thereby directs behaviour.

In his landmark book *Aging Well* (Vaillant, 2003), Vaillant concludes that the mastery and embodiment of Generativity is the best predictor for happiness and success in later life; from enduring and happy marriages to good health and vibrant, fulfilling participation in a wide range of work and social activities. His research is based solidly on the results of three ground-breaking studies, which include two by Harvard Medical School. These followed over 824 male and female subjects over the course of 60 years, from their teens to their 80s. The heart of his theory is that an individual's personal history impacts less on their long-term happiness than the attitudes and behaviours they adopt and the specific lifestyle choices they make. So positive-thinking, happy, generative individuals live longer.

To my mind the cult of Success, as personified by the ideal of the thrusting 40-something, has a lot to answer for. It is far too simplistic, and far too much a one-size-fits-all argument for a time of life when we are actually becoming more sophisticated in our understanding of our self. Unfortunately, as there are few role models in our sights for later-career anyway, anything which comes across as different to the hard-nosed, competitive leadership style, particularly if it doesn't *look* physically like the 40-something, runs into ingrained, conditioned prejudices. It's just not the 'norm'.

There is the fear perhaps, as described by Gail Sheehy, of the 'paradox that as we reach our prime, we also see there is a place where it finishes'. I have come across so many high-powered executives who only feel safe if they are acknowledged as sticking to that traditional 'norm'. Perhaps they are the ones who still have the same haircut as when they took their first job? Or prefer to believe that if they do not appear to change, change itself will not catch up with them? Are they the men who, in ever increasing numbers and in spite of teasing women for years for doing the same thing, are taking to dying their greying hair with impossibly brassy shades of brown?

I distinctly recall a presentation I was asked to run on later-career for a small group of professional services Partners. I could see a couple of the older Partners looking distinctly uncomfortable, and fidgeting in their seats as I described the attributes and strengths of each phase, and got to the subject of Generativity. They were at pains to make me aware that I wouldn't find many of their Partners losing their ego even in their 60s, or interested in much apart from their own billings and the profits. It is an attitude or, better expressed, a *fear* that I hear very often. It is as if we are conditioned to see life as a choice constrained between 'EITHER/OR', rather than as an opportunity opened up by 'AND'.

The Role Model issue also comes into play here again. If we go along with the adult development theory, we actually will have seen people behaving generatively. Probably these were among our grandparents and their friends. We are likely to have been the direct beneficiaries of it, as their grandchildren. We have observed them being patient, humble, caring to others, long-term thinkers, people in whom we felt safe to confide, people we felt cared about who we were and what we did, etc.

We have probably unconsciously labelled that 'what grandparents do', and put it in the 'family' compartment, well away from anything to do with work or leadership. Unfortunately that can lead to us thinking that because grandparents do that sort of thing, and because we don't see their age group normally in a work environment, *that sort of approach doesn't have a place in the work environment*. It is a very misguided assumption. Reframe it! *Anyone* showing 21st century-style leadership attributes such as humility, patience and care for the world at large needs to be appreciated, studied and emulated – not patronised.

I tested out this theory with Edward, who had previously spoken with me several years ago about the insights he got from Daniel Petre's book *Father Time* (Petre, 2005) on how fatherhood shapes one's responses to the world and how we act as leaders, and how we can harness that. He now has three young grandchildren, two girls and a boy:

> I think you are right. With my grandchildren, for example, I find myself listening in a way I never did with my own children. Somehow it's not so important to have to be 'right' on every subject with them, as it seemed to be to me with my children. I don't feel I always have to give advice, like I used to, either. Often it seems to be about just offering a safe space and being someone who takes them seriously.
>
> That hit home to me in a rather special way one day when my grandson was coping with his parents' divorce. He was confused, sad, a bit angry and also unsettled about having to spend time in two homes instead of just one. If that had been ten years ago, I think I would have handled it very differently. I can imagine myself going in, grasping the 'task' which was the logistics of shuttling between two houses, and focused in on that. I could have told myself I was being helpful, but I'd really have been avoiding the emotional aspect.
>
> Even more than that, I'd have been protecting myself more than I'd have been protecting him because I guessed there was something that was going

on for him which a large part of me simply didn't want to hear. He was angry with his mother, my daughter, for being the one he felt split up his nice, happy, safe home. And I knew it would hurt me terribly hearing him say things about my darling girl, who was always daddy's girl and could never put a foot wrong in my eyes.

This time I just listened. It wasn't really the shuttling back and forth which he wanted to talk about (although we did eventually end up with some pretty dandy ideas about what to do about school books and sports clothes, etc. once we'd got the other stuff out of the way). He wanted to talk about how he felt and offer up his opinions on what was going on. He didn't want advice – and I realized I couldn't have given him any anyway. If I'd have given him platitudes they would just have shut him up, and that's what he definitely didn't need or deserve.

I learned so much from that afternoon. I learned that a little boy of 9 knows far more about the pain of a divorce than I do. I've never been through one, how could I? And I learnt far more about the whole picture than by just seeing it through my daughter's eyes. And I really hope I was therefore far better equipped to be of support to them both, and my ex-son-in-law for that matter.

I think I've grown into that, being more inclusive and open-minded in a way, as I've got older. I know they say the older you get, the more stuck in your ways and your opinions you are, but I actually see the opposite happening. When I give away my need to be right and know all the answers – yet offer a safe place for people to explore and offer their opinions and suggestions.

Could I see how taking that approach would work well in business? Of course I can. Could I say I always do that now? No – but I'm conscious of the need to work on it.

It is definitely worth checking whether we carry those assumptions, as they might lead us to filter out excellent qualities displayed by 'grandparents', merely because we haven't had experience of their age group in a leadership context. Such generative attitudes and behaviour are surely very much needed in leaders in the 21st century environment.

The match with Level 5 leadership

In fact, what strikes me most strongly is the parallel between the characteristics of generative behaviour and the Level 5 leadership described by Jim Collins' masterwork *Good to Great* (Collins, 2001). As he puts it, 'Level 5 leaders channel their ego needs away from themselves and into the larger goal of building a great company. It is not that Level 5 leaders have no ego or self-interest. Indeed they are incredibly ambitious. But their ambition is first and foremost for the institution, not themselves.'

Try translating Level 5 leadership as Generativity, for '*institution*' read '*the world*'. It becomes far more impressive – far more *Significant*.

A great proponent of that type of leadership, and someone more than happy to claim it as generative behaviour, is John McFarlane, former CEO at ANZ Bank. He was coming to the end of his term there, and what could be retirement if he chose it to be, when I spoke to him. On his watch the bank had raised its profits and performance year on year, at the same time as raising its reputation. This had been in direct contrast to a number of other competitors in the market which, during the same period, had found themselves embroiled in scandals around currency trading and sweeping redundancies due to moving volume work offshore.

For John, the key to high performance in individuals and in an institution is a sense of purpose, a disposition to service. I asked him how he saw his brief:

> I think I've been able to do this job with far more wisdom than at 40. At this point in my career I know I have greater insight, better judgement and just greater all-round effectiveness than I've ever had before. I'm here to help make a difference to the bank, and to banking in the broader context. . . . It also matters to me to be a contributing member of society – beyond banking. It's important to have that sense of Meaning, as it's Meaning which sparks energy. Because of that, I think I've felt happier in my work than I've ever done. It's something about *having a sense of Significance* above and beyond results and personal 'Success'.

In our typologies in the following Chapter 3, mastery of Generativity is most apparent in the Coach figure. It turns Confucius, Moses and even King Lear on their heads, because instead of suggesting that the right format is for the young to care for the old, it celebrates the opportunity (for that is how this extra half a lifetime can be grasped) for the older to nurture the younger.

To me the most exciting and stimulating aspect of Generativity is that it is about far more than wisdom and the treasure house of knowledge built up over the years (and which are usually achieved more by pure osmosis than conscious effort). When I hear people referring to the 'wisdom' of those in later-career it sounds so passive. Even aloof. Generativity is about an attitude of mind, a pro-active response to circumstances, a way of being which nourishes abundance and, as Professor Sharon Moore, when Professor of Strategy at The University of Western Sydney, put it so succinctly, 'Aims to provide a larger, tastier pie for all'.

So what's not to like about Generativity?!?

I have met quite a few executives who feel it is incumbent upon them to disparage anything to do with psychologists, particularly about adult development. Supposedly too touchy-feely perhaps? I wonder if that is only because some of the findings make them personally uncomfortable and confronted? The paradox I have found is that most of those same people, with their parental hat on, eagerly read and support the theories of child development experts. There is no logical difference to be made.

We must be wary that we do not muddle *physical* with *emotional* and *attitudinal* development. It is undeniable that certain physical functions deteriorate with age, but this starts from as young as one's 20s. A certain number of men are bald by 22, and a larger number find they need spectacles for reading by somewhere in their early 40s. Bad backs and creaky knees hit sportsmen not long after their playing peaks. A bit of physical decline is certainly not confined to the 60s and beyond.

As we will explore further in Chapter 4, extensive research has been undertaken which has proven that older workers are not the frail sickness-prone types of our stereotyping. In fact they are shown to be hardier, more resilient, more committed to soldiering on and indeed better at prevention of avoidable illness than their younger counterparts.

The point is, though, that physical development (and within that I would class the physical functioning of the brain) tends inexorably towards ultimate decline and cessation of bodily function.

On the other hand, emotional and attitudinal development surely errs towards *continuing improvement* and progress. Especially as it is a 'build-on' type of development. By this I mean that it can be viewed as an ascending staircase, as in Erikson's model, or as in Carol Gilligan's version from her work *In a Different Voice* (Gilligan, 1993), in which she likens development to a stone dropped into water. It produces ever-expanding ripples, with each older ripple encompassing, but not obliterating, the circle coming from the next ripple.

The benefits and beauty accruing from *claiming* one's Generativity in the Second Half is that it both encompasses and *transcends* career consolidation and all the excellent qualities and responses of our earlier developmental history. We do not have to give up anything from before, but embrace it and build upon it ever more knowingly and effectively.

Since the early philosophers it has been assumed that man's essential nature is continually evolving towards improvement and progression. Aristotle claimed that as individuals we have the capacity to advance morally and behaviourally, affecting society for the better as we do so. Then as the culture of our society progresses, it influences the individual for the good too, creating a virtuous circle or in fact a virtuous spiral.

This is reflected in the Spiral Dynamics theories of Don Beck and Chris Cowan (Beck and Cowan, 2005), and taken up by Ken Wilber (Wilber, 2000), at whose base is the belief that as individuals and as species we have the capacity to encompass and transcend other levels as we grow in intellectual, moral and behavioural sophistication. Spiral Dynamics argues that human nature is not fixed: human beings evolve or develop through eight major colour-coded waves of consciousness. These develop from Beige (Archaic-Instinctual, regarding basic survival) through Purple, Red, Orange, Green and Yellow to Turquoise (Universal-Holistic, regarding integrative energies). According to Beck and Cowan, these conceptual models are organised around 'memes'. In Spiral Dynamics, the term 'meme' refers to a core value system, acting as an organising principle, which expresses itself through memes (self-propagating ideas, habits or cultural practices).

Similar to Gilligan's view of adult psychological development, Spiral Dynamics states that every new wave of consciousness and development *includes* and *transcends* all previous waves.

It can be interpreted as an explanation of historical societal development, on one level, and as an aspirational model for the individual on another. It is a fascinating theory to explore, and I would recommend Ken Wilber's works in particular for those interested to know more. Whilst not totally germane to explore it more deeply in this context, it offers the attractive argument that we all have the capacity to continue to develop our level of consciousness as we grow and age. There are distinct parallels between the higher, more integrated meme levels within it and the, rather less complex, concept of Generativity.

So, going back to the Erikson-inspired model, I fail to see any argument for holding on to the more ego-based consolidation phase any more than one would wish to remain in the tortured search for getting the balance of intimacy right as a young adult. Like intimacy, which Vaillant paraphrases as the task of living with another person/people in an interdependent, reciprocal, committed fashion, Generativity simply needs practice until the benefits of dealing with it become second or, rather, one's new nature.

John Kotre, in his work *Outliving the Self* (Kotre, 1984), describes the work of Generativity as 'investing one's substance in forms of life and work that will outlive the self'. Mastery of it takes one who is successful into a realm beyond – into Significance. It is not about a dutiful burgher leaving a worthy legacy, either in the form of money or assets amassed. It concerns finding a meaning and purpose to one's existence, which extends not just to one's short-term satisfaction and gain, but to the long term, and into the fabric of others as individuals and as institutions. It is to the 21st century Holy Grail of Sustainability, what Success is to Quarterly Results.

Erikson himself also saw Generativity, and the later years, as a 'widening of the social radius'. Not only does this indicate a movement away from the selfish and purely ego-focused ambition of the consolidation phase, but it offers a new and exciting bridge to the stewardship inherent in Sustainability.

Integrating Generativity with personal career sustainability

Sharon Jackson, my friend, colleague and founder of Carlton CSR, shares my views on the link between corporate sustainability and career sustainability, and the opportunity for both sides of that equation to be more proactive in harnessing the qualities of Generativity in later-leadership:

> Through my work with organisations and customised executive development, it is my deeply held view that sustainable business activities should be operationalised from inside the business.
>
> Organisations committing to sustainable, responsible, community-supporting business must realise that they should start at the heart of their organisation through ensuring the sustainability of the knowledge and skills in their own workforce, through Extended Careers. Rather than taking the view of making allowances for older workers and leaders the opposite stance should be taken by actively developing and harnessing the attributes of Generativity which are likely to blossom in later-career. This brings a wealth of diverse knowledge, skill and commitment.

These potentially 'Generative Leaders' are people who have witnessed first hand the cumulative effects of climate change, waste and pollution, corporate malfeasance and the continued global trend of disparity between rich and poor, plus they have the skills and experience to drive organisational change to embrace responsible business principles as business as usual.

Successful leaders and managers in later-career have usually developed a deeper understanding of the issues of sustainability and are often more deeply in tune with a sense of their own integrity and personal values than they have ever been before in their lives. They tend to be well travelled, well read and have a diverse range of life experiences to draw from, which means that they can usually bring a pragmatic and measured view in respect to ethical decision making, a cornerstone of responsible business.

From my experience, it seems that many CSR and sustainability initiatives do not take advantage of the generative traits which those in later career have grown into, and which everyone could gain from to have them developed further.

There is much debate about the responsibility of a business, where does that responsibility start and end. This particular issue highlights the importance of a business's responsibility to itself to engage the most effective talent and also to the community of successful people who are still in their prime of performance, with a wealth of knowledge, experience but are stereotyped by their birth date.

Looking around the world today it is stimulating as well as heartening to see examples of Generativity, creating new role models to aspire to in the Second Half. Two former Presidents have been demonstrating it through their books and global involvement in the mega issues of relieving poverty, world peace and the environment – Jimmy Carter and Bill Clinton. Even more famously, the slightly younger Al Gore is both Nobel Laureate and Oscar-winner for his campaigning around climate change and environmental degradation.

A common misconception about later-career and Generativity is that it just means moving into the NFP sector or into unpaid voluntary work. This is definitely not the case. A new generation of what have been termed 'old-erpreneurs' are setting up a wide range of different businesses but, judging from sites like www.primebusinessclub.com (PRIME: The Prince's Initiative for Mature Enterprise set up by HRH The Prince of Wales to assist over-50s become self-employed or set up a business), a very large percentage of them are purposely eco-friendly businesses as they step out of years in traditional transnationals. In the UK a Yellow Pages survey in 2007 noted that over-50s who are setting up their own businesses are contributing £24.4 billion to the economy each year and account for one in six start-up businesses. The survey also indicated that this group forms the most stable and successful demographic for new businesses.

That is not to say that NFPs and NGOs do not have an appeal for later-career leaders too, making a change in their work environment. Organisations like Prime Timers (www.primetimers.org.uk) are expanding as generative Second-Halfers choose to move into the Third Sector instead of retirement. As well as providing consulting expertise to charities, the organisation recruits 'Prime Timers' (Second-Halfers) into the sector to offer their skills in interim management, mentor and trustee roles as well as full- and part-time specialists, and provides a very practical preparation to help commercial-world executives transition smoothly and successfully into a different sphere.

Generativity offers our corporate world and the community at large the type of subtle skills so extraordinarily necessary for 21st century operational success. In addition, it is synonymous with the yearning to 'reach beyond' and to truly make a difference to the world, and being socially responsible.

Lastly, and as the ultimate retort to those who might say, 'So what's in it for me? Why Mr Nice Guy?', all three of the Harvard Medical School longitudinal studies mentioned earlier confirmed that mastery of Generativity tripled the chances that the decade of the 70s would be a time for happiness and fulfilment, not of despair and lost hope.

***

DEVELOPING THE GAMEPLAN:
Claim your Generativity

Questions & activities to help you test
out your attitudes towards Generativity
and explore what that means to you in your
life and how you live it

1. What shape is your career?

The most familiar model for a career in the 20th century is the ladder. A
major problem with that has always been, 'Where to next?' once someone
gets to the top rung. This can happen to young, successful entrepreneurs
who achieve pretty much all they've ever dreamed of, then lose a sense of
purpose. But it is far more common for those reaching the later stages of
their career, after a lifetime of climbing the rungs.

How much does your career resemble the ladder?
Where do you consider you are on the ladder at this point in your life?
How do you feel about that image?
How does it feel to be where you are?

If you don't see your career as a ladder, what image comes to mind
instead?

In either case, what shape do you see your career/activities as over the
next five years?
How would you like it to look?
How does it compare with the last five years? And the five before
that?

What are you looking forward to over the next five years?
What are you not looking forward to over the next five years?

2. Perspectives on career phases

In this chapter we have looked at a particular model of adult development life stages. The age groupings are obviously quite broad, and some people will spend longer in some stages than others. It can also be very useful and revealing to look into each stage and try to work out one's own subsets. In our seminars we ask participants to look back at their lives, particularly in career terms, and divide it up into their own idea of phases.

Draw another life line below, as in Chapter 1.

Mark on it what you see as your own career phases to date. They can be any length and may overlap.

> What name/descriptor would you give to each of these phases?
> How would you characterise yourself in each of these phases?
> What did you like, and what did you dislike about yourself in each phase?
> How much control do you feel you had about each of them?
> What did you learn from each phase?
> In what ways do you feel you have changed over the years?
> In what ways have you stayed the same?

Here is an example:

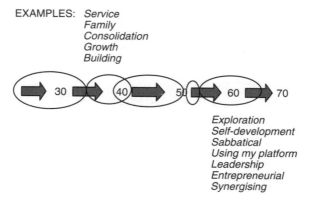

Figure 2.2 Recognising and naming career phases

Mark on the same life line what phases you see ahead.

> Do you have names/descriptors for future career phases?
> What do they mean to you?
> How much control do you feel you will have over them?

3. LAGOM – what is 'enough?'

If the Second Half is to be truly liveable and fulfilling, the right balance needs to be struck between material and emotional needs.

What is your definition of **enough**?

> *Finances*
> How much is enough?
> Do you see it as a monetary amount?
> Or do you see it as 'enough *in order to* . . .'?
>
> *What makes life worth living?*
> Do you have enough of what *you* feel makes life worth living?
> How would you rate yourself on the following? (Score 1–10, minimum–maximum):
>
> **Fun**
> **Health**
> **Laughter**
> **Love**
> **Friendship**
> **Self-expression**
> **Sense of meaning/purpose**
> **Time**
> **Passionate interest**
> **Sense of belonging/community**
> **Physical expression**
>
> What will you do to increase your score on each, to ensure you have 'enough'?

4. Generativity and role models

If you are to claim your Generativity and use it as a quality of strength in the Second Half, it helps to begin by identifying role models for it. You can be your own role model too, by noticing where you have displayed some of the traits of *service above ego*, *shaping a legacy*, *taking a community stance*, *showing empathetic leadership*, *caring and guiding those who follow in your footsteps*, and so on.

Who do you see as role models for Generativity?
What is it about those people that resonates most with you?
In what ways do they demonstrate Generativity?

How much do you identify with the concept of Generativity yourself?
In what ways do you feel you are like your role models?
In what ways do they show up how you are unlike them?

What situations can you think of in which you have demonstrated a generative approach?
Are there ways in which you would like to use this more? If so, what would that look like?
Are there any obstacles to you in doing this? If so, what are they and how might you get over them?

What can you do today or tomorrow which would demonstrate and live out your generative approach?

3

Becoming a Second Half hero
OR
Create your own role model

Until the generation which has just moved into Second Half, the majority of the population have lived neither long nor actively in their years beyond middle age. Over 50s have always previously been a minority group. That is the simple reason why it is so hard to find attractive and inspirational role models for 'winning in our Second Halves', and why we so often default to the unattractive, generic stereotypes.

The upside is that we are at an opportunity-rich point in history, at which we are the ones with responsibility to create those new models. When I was interviewing for this book the question which the leaders and top executives from all over the world found hardest to answer was, '*Who do you most admire for what they are doing in their 60s and 70s? Who are your positive role models for that age?*'

Over 80% told me that their minds went completely blank. When they could come up with names, over 50% found that what they were admiring was what that individual had done or been *earlier* in life rather than when they were beyond 60. The images which came to their mind were predominantly negative, not positive.

Minorities and typologies

The one role model who was mentioned again and again, however, was Nelson Mandela. A Second Half hero if ever there was one, coming back to victory after an exceedingly tough First Half. Mandela is also an icon to the Black community worldwide, a minority community in most cases, which should make us reflect on minorities and the obstacles they encounter which can thwart their influence and success.

The philosopher Aristotle was one of the first to realise that without role models or some sort of positive 'template' it is very hard to shape our own thoughts on what even the *possibilities* are for individuals. What minorities share is a shortage of powerful role models when breaking new ground and particularly around leadership. Minorities do not have the comfort of the numbers of being mainstream or 'the norm'. Minorities have to look to the exceptions, the UberHeroes like Mandela or Thatcher or Mother Teresa rather than a smorgasbord of local, personally known role models and potential mentors.

The older age-group still falls into this sort of minority category too. As Betty Friedan in *The Fountain of Age* points out (Friedan, 2006), because like women, blacks and the disabled this group has been invisible in the media until now, so there is precious little to look to and identify with.

The good news, of course, is that minorities can foster and create new role models. And, given the experience, expertise and general smartness of those currently in leadership roles in later-career or heading towards it, one would trust that those role models can indeed come confidently into being.

I am a great believer in the aspect of the Law of Attraction, insomuch as we bring towards us that which we think about. That means grumpiness begets more grumpiness but positive thinking attracts positive results. So when formulating any sort of role models it is far more useful to focus on what we *want* rather than what we *don't want*. Yet, at the same time, it is worthwhile to be conscious of what we want to avoid too or we would fail to learn from experiences.

For that reason I believe it is valuable to look at some of the later-career typologies which exist. In the seminars and workshops I conduct, participants find it revealing and helpful to discuss them among themselves. (See www.CGAcademy.org or winnersinthesecondhalf.com for details of future events.) Some examples are more positive and compelling than others, but there are elements of behaviours within each with which individuals are likely to identify in themselves. Becoming more conscious of that identification can immediately help to either modify or promote that behaviour.

In addition, we take similar mini case studies and brainstorm on the various permutations of outcomes for these types. What are the likely ramifications of certain actions? What are the potential trade-offs? Will circumstances impact substantially enough to change responses?

As in any form of scenario exploration, the benefit is in going beyond the first thing which comes to mind. The immediate response is often the conditioned reflex (as in the first case study following) as opposed to fuller reflection based on life experience. Without the commitment, and time, to devote to exploring the full range of possible outcomes, we are deprived of a broader vision and insight.

Through the conversations I've had, and through the research I've read and carried out myself, I have developed seven major typologies, set in the form of sporting metaphors, for those of us in or approaching our Second Half.

The ones which appear to have most trouble tackling their Second Halves can be characterised as:

- The Defender
- The Referee
- On the Benches

Other typologies have evolved to take a much more positive approach to setting up, entering and living out their Second Halves:

- The Captain
- The Coach
- The Olympic Athlete
- The Master

Let's start off with the three less well-equipped for the challenges of a new half of the game.

Case Study: The Defender

Which matches do you remember from the last World Cup? Unless you are a die-hard partisan, not those dominated by Defenders. Not the 0–0 draws. Not the Second Halves where nothing much happened because each side was concentrating on holding on to the score in the First Half.

As one ex-Premier League goalkeeper I once met assured me, his least enjoyable games were those where he took more passes back from his own defenders than goal attempts by the opposition.

It may be a strategy for advancing to the Quarter Finals . . . but is it a viable strategy for *living fully* in your own Second Half?

Defenders tend to have careers which have been long-tenure, with little exposure to change. Being risk-averse by nature, they seem to resemble defenders in a soccer match: unlikely to score goals or be flashy players and more concerned with stopping the other side from winning, or focused on minimising a loss.

This type has the capacity to be a good planner, but often sabotages himself by being deep into denial. They would prefer to feel that tomorrow will be pretty much the same as today – so it can better be kept under control. Consciously or unconsciously they will often avoid looking too closely at what might turn out to be an uncomfortably 'different' set of circumstances. Whilst desperate to feel that they have everything under control (and even more desperate to try to *show* that they have), their need to hold tight to a status quo often leads them to make errors of judgement and 'play for time' instead.

In sport, great defenders win by thinking ahead and using their heuristics to forecast where the game will go next, and what to look out for. The more mediocre ones show far less imagination, and are content to be reactive. They also have the greater propensity to lash out aggressively when challenged or taken by surprise. And of course bad players deny their own responsibility and blame those further upfield: 'If that corner had only been cleared properly, they couldn't have got through'. It is everybody else's problem, not theirs. In contrast, the best acknowledge their responsibility, but then move on.

Donald knew me through my Search work. He was slightly reticent to be interviewed, telling me, 'I really don't see the point of a book like this for someone like myself. I'm fine about my next steps.' He was 58 and he had had a solid, if unremarkable career culminating in becoming Managing Partner, a role from which he was just about to retire. Right from the start of our conversation his body language veered from defensive (folded arms and crossed legs) to aggressive (leaning forward, raised voice, sarcasm).

'I suppose you are looking for people who want to have a major seachange. Or who don't know what to do with themselves. I won't be any use to you in that.

I've enough to live on comfortably and I'll be taking up Board positions and spending time with my family.'

I asked him how difficult he thought it would be to find suitable NED positions, given that his present business had policies forbidding him taking those roles when still in employment with them, and added that genuinely interesting Boards were probably in far shorter supply than most people believed.

I was genuinely surprised when he snapped back, *'What, don't you think I'm good enough or something?'* I shared with him that my experience in Search was that often one was very popular when at the top of the tree, and with significant influence within the firm and industry, and that once 'retired' even the best individuals could be overlooked and forgotten unless there had been some solid ground-preparation for a Director's career in advance. *'Well, I'm not a Schmoozer, if that's what you mean. I have strong contacts.'*

Continuing, I tried to find out what other options he had, or was still considering, *'Why should I think of anything else? I've got a lot to offer Boards. I've seen a lot of other people nowhere near as qualified go on them. Lots of them.'* But had he actively considered other options? *'No! What point are you trying to make?'* He was clearly getting upset and frustrated with my line of questioning.

Perhaps most telling of all was the response when I asked, *'And what do your family think about you spending more time with them? What have you discussed?'* There was a pause, a slightly blank stare as if this was something he had never considered and had come totally out of left field. *'Well . . . we haven't really spoken about it in much detail yet I suppose.'*

I would have loved to have heard his wife's interpretation of the situation.

Two or three years on

Have a look at the following questions and gauge what you think the likely outcomes are for Donald and his Defender stance regarding his situation two or three years down the track.

There are no 'right answers' – just some that are more comfortable to live with than others. All of the options have been observed arising in similar real-life situations.

1. NED roles

   (a) Several, on fascinating Boards.

   (b) Several, on rather boring, frustrating Boards.

(c) Not enough of either to keep himself consistently occupied.

(d) Disillusionment with the activities of being a NED.

2. **Other options**

(a) A realisation that there may be more to life than Board work, but no idea how to go about working out what that might be.

(b) A sense of futility and lack of fulfilment, but too much pride to look at alternatives.

(c) A couple of frustrating years and heart-searching, followed by a move into a new area of occupation (e.g. setting up own company, hands-on volunteering, retraining as homeopath, casual article writer, etc.).

(d) Reconnecting with his old firm to find activity, paid or unpaid, with them.

3. **Family life**

(a) His wife has been fully, seamlessly in synch with all the things he wanted to do together.

(b) He had been so used to his wife organising their social life that he had not realised how hard it is to 'make things happen'. He felt depressed, isolated and lost self-confidence.

(c) His wife had very different ideas about what his 'retirement' would look like and, with more time on their hands than ever before, they began to argue more than ever before.

(d) Taking his 'boss' behaviours into the home environment upset the balance of their relationship. She is seriously considering divorce.

Case Study: The Referee

A referee is certainly part of a game – but can't quite be called a player. His or her key role is to police the rules of the game and make sure it never gets out of hand. But it is never 'his' game. He can certainly ensure it goes smoothly, even memorably. Yet this person is unlikely ever to have the rush of genuine involvement, unlike even the most mediocre player on either team – because ultimately it is not *their* game, and they do not share in the thrill of engaging with the emotion of win or lose. Yes, a referee is an integral part of a game, but who ever remembers the name of a referee? Or has ever swapped bubblegum cards of referees?

Those that fall into the Referee typology are often the stalwart, sensible souls who have spent their whole careers in a single firm or industry sector. They often have marvellous nest-eggs amassed in later-career, and many less financially assured people will look at them and think how lucky they are and how well set up they are by that stage.

Yet these are the ones who, when asked to explain the path of their career, will realise that they only got into it to please someone else. Often their parents. Or, indirectly, their parents but via the sage advice of a family friend – usually in that suggested business themselves! And they have stayed there, particularly in the Professional Services field, because they were quite good at it and nothing else seemed to offer as much monetary and tenure security during a time when they had a growing family to support, etc., etc. Not surprisingly many spouses buy into the glorious sensibleness of it too, and become the person whom the 'Referee' wants to please instead, replacing parental approval.

The kick, though, is often at the end. 'What else can I do now, since I've never done anything else?' is a complaint I often hear. It is made all the more tragic if it is followed by, 'And, frankly, I've never much enjoyed it anyway'.

The happiest and most successful *beyond* their career in Referee mode are invariably those who have scoped and planned and looked forward to some version of the Monty Python catchphrase 'And now for something completely different', and are not caught unawares and holding someone else's Rule Book in their hands.

As I heard from Eric, who has umpired at Wimbledon: 'It's fine being an umpire and adjudicating someone else's matches. But I'd go mad if I didn't know I'd be going out on the court myself at the weekend too!'

Andrew was someone I coached for a while. I always had the image of him as a Referee to his own 'game'. It was as if he was not actually 'in' the game, but somehow standing apart. He said himself that he felt he had never really fitted the mould, in the somewhat cut-throat atmosphere of one of the more competitive law firms. Like it was actually someone else's game, and he was simply supervising the activities. And indeed, in common with a sad number of those who go dutifully into a 'safe' profession in their early 20s, and stay there, he told me that he had been persuaded into it by a friend of the family, a Senior Partner in his first law firm.

'I really wanted to be in Social Work of some form or another. Even active politics. I wanted to make a difference. But my parents felt it would be a waste of my education to go into something that didn't pay, and which didn't have some sort of kudos. I didn't want to disappoint them. Law seemed the sensible thing to do. And I've been a success in it.' (I wish you could have heard the lacklustre way he spoke that last sentence. The tone was totally in contradiction to the content.)

He was very much into the 'Rules of the Game' too. I couldn't help but wonder whether this was Andrew's way of keeping _himself_ under control. When I first met him he was taking redundancy from the law firm. (I was never actually sure whether it was a 'did he go or was he pushed' scenario.)

Neither the Managing Partner nor the HR Director had any idea what Andrew was going to do – but they knew that he had plenty of money and no family ties. Tellingly, I thought, the (male) Managing Partner felt that it would all therefore be plain sailing for the man, whereas the (female) HR Director believed that those very issues could be more problems than plus points for him.

As part of my work with executives in the later stages of their career and particularly with those who have spent the major part of their career in one sector or function, we explore future options. (See www.CGAcademy.org or winnersinthesecondhalf.com for details of future events and public workshops.) Using a number of practical and proven methodologies and exercises we brain-storm creatively and broadly together about what the future options might be. The aim is to go as wide, far and uninhibitedly as possible so as to maximise the opportunities for new thoughts, extrapolations, serendipitous connections and what-ifs to arise. Only then do we begin the process of honing down the list and establishing gameplans. Without that step it is human nature, especially for the congenitally risk-averse, to stay within their comfort zones and eschew anything which looks new and unfamiliar.

But Andrew was by far the hardest person I'd ever had to work with on that. As referee he was constantly blowing the whistle on himself: 'People like me don't do X' and 'I couldn't possibly do that, after being seen in a role like this!' or 'I don't think the firm would be very pleased with me if I went off and did that'. Even, 'My poor mother would go mad if I suggested that'. He was like one of those ultra-punctilious referees who constantly interrupt the flow of the game for minor infringements. He verged on being the type of referee who'd take the Rule

Book, read one out and then menace: 'Don't do that!' before the player had even moved a muscle or shown any intention of infringing.

He was vigorously trying to cut off and dismiss his options before they had so much as seen the light of day. His excuses were always what psychologists term self-limiting beliefs (SLBs). As topics came up like 'Councillor', 'NFP Head', 'Academic' or 'International role somewhere', his body language would change. He put his hands on his head, in a typical gesture signifying, 'I don't want to let this feeling/option/emotion out'. The self-limiting beliefs he had unconsciously fostered over the years were causing him to show those options a Red Card. 'Get them off the field!'

Through repeating the exercise, in several different versions, it was clear that his major passions and interests could be found in the areas of academia and community service. There were literally dozens of options he could explore to finally choose a selection to try out for size. But time after time he cut them off at their mere mention. 'Offside!'

I worried about him once he finally left. While he remains as referee to his own life, it looks as if his own Second Half will still be spent simply running up and down the field, part of someone else's game.

Two or three years on

What may be happening in Andrew's life once he finally moves out of his long-tenure position? What are his likely options for response?

As you reflect on the questions, consider where you may see yourself as similar or as different to Andrew and his responses.

1. **Self-limiting beliefs**
    (a) Andrew will carry them with him forever.
    (b) He will challenge them if he begins to find life too dull without a structure or any meaningful personal interactions.
    (c) Once his parents have died he will feel freer to re-examine his SLBs and make new decisions.
    (d) He may find that once he has left the Law field, other acquaintances or friends – in fields in which he has greater rapport – may actively approach him about options and cause him to challenge his own preconceptions.

2. **Activities**
   (a) Andrew will take up a few occasional consulting roles in the area in which he had specialised.
   (b) He will not work at all, nor get involved in other activities, in case they are perceived as 'the wrong ones'.
   (c) He may be surprised by actually being asked by others outside the firm, and among his broader contacts, to take on roles he may have dismissed himself out of hand.
   (d) Andrew will develop a portfolio of activities. Some will be connected to law, but others will touch on areas such as academia, community or politics.

Case Study: On the Benches

My mental image of this type is someone on the benches of some fast-moving ball game. It may be soccer, it may be rugby, it may be baseball, it may be Aussie Rules. It's no World Series which comes to mind though. More like the Substitute Bench of an Under-10s game.

You can picture it. The ball is going up and down the field. It looks such fun to all the kids. The eagerness, the impatience, the hope, the despair but ultimately the sheer frustration is all writ large on those little faces. Because at that age the emotions are so close to the surface. So very lived, so very vivid because those little players haven't yet learnt how to repress and stifle them.

'Oh please can I join in, Sir! Just let me have a kick of the ball. Pleeeease! Don't just leave me sitting here.'

I began to see, metaphorically, that image on the faces of many of the candidates I was meeting in the Search process when I was still in that business. 'Don't leave me just sitting here!' They might look calm and sensibly suited, but inside they were yearning to be let on to the pitch. To play a stormer of a game in the Second Half. The hope, the impatience to actually be allowed out onto that field to play their hearts out before the final whistle blows. They've trained for it. They've looked forward to the opportunity. . . .

But you know what? The ultimate frustration is that there are many great players sitting on the benches in later-career and beyond *simply because they have no idea what to do with themselves*. They feel themselves sitting on the sidelines of life, somewhere into the Second Half and dreadfully anxious that time is running out.

Perhaps this group is the most widespread of all. I've come across them at all levels and in all sorts of organisations, as well as after they have left. Wonderful people, and exceptional talents, who have either forgotten or simply haven't thought enough in advance about what's needed to go out there and win in the Second Half. Sadly, for many, towards later-career and looking beyond, it's sometimes like seeing them turn up at a match – but with no idea what game is being played, and no kit. Of course they can't join in!

And why didn't they look it up beforehand, and come along prepared? The usual excuse is, 'Too busy!' or 'I'll work it out when I get there'. In particularly high-pressure roles, where there may be a sense of burn-out and running on empty, there is also often a tendency to concentrate on running away *from* a stressful and often unfulfilling situation. That person takes it for granted that they know where they are running *to*, but in actual fact they often haven't a clue.

Henry was a big name in Investment Banking. He had had a highly successful career, and was a well-known figure in his field internationally. He used to love the cut-and-thrust and intellectual stimulation of the business, the up-close contact with clients and deal partners, and the power inherent in achievement and his position within the firm.

However, for the last three or four years he had been feeling far more stressed than usual. Not because of workload, nor even performance expectations, but more because of feeling less and less in touch and connected with the new CEO and some of the new team he had brought in with him. Henry found himself somewhat depressed, more complaining than he liked himself to be, and anxious to find any excuse to take a longer holiday or a long weekend to get away from the office. His wife told him he was becoming a grump and chastised him for working too hard. As an antidote to his discomfort his thoughts occasionally turned to when he might leave the company. It was a comfortingly vague picture in his mind – still several years away, built of random ideas of more golf, longer lunches and travelling with his wife and possibly grandchildren.

He was completely taken by surprise one day when the Chairman urged him, very diplomatically and persuasively, to take the ample retirement package that was on offer. Henry felt slightly offended but relieved at the same time. He didn't feel any less vigorous than he had ever done, and he was assured it had nothing to do with his performance. But he certainly did feel that a break from the long hours and general pressure would do him good.

The first 15 months or so were fine. He improved his golf handicap, he visited Italy for the first time with his wife, took her and their twin granddaughters on a cruise and he even oversaw the building of a small extension to their kitchen. He did not have as many long lunches as he would have liked or expected, because his old lunching partners were either still working full-time or were retired and living right across town:

> It was on my second birthday after leaving the company that I realized I was bored – and that I felt useless. I had no compelling reason to get out of bed in the morning. At least at the office I had a reason – even if I hated that reason. And no-one was calling me. I went from having a diary where my PA had to book people in weeks in advance, to days upon days of clear calendar. It wasn't just that the lack of calls meant not much social or intellectual life. I was confused – and hurt too, I suppose – that none of my old cronies seemed to have time for me. I could understand why – I was no USE to them. I could understand that on one level, but it still bruised my ego.
>
> Then when my wife starting rolling her eyes every time I suggested another trip, and complained I was upsetting her routine and her time with friends, it felt like the ultimate betrayal. It seemed everyone else had a life – except me!

Henry had gone from being the star player to a spectator in a matter of months. He said he knew exactly how David Beckham felt when he was dropped as England Captain and left out of the team.

> Yes, I know I should have expected all that. It seems so obvious now. I was so intent on escaping the office, as it had become so draining and depressing to me that I didn't think about what would come after. And I made the assumption that I had all the time in the world to start thinking about it, which of course turned out not to be the case. Mind you, in all honesty, I don't think I ever would have got round to putting much thought into it. I just made the assumption that it couldn't possibly be worse. I still can't say it was worse – but I can't say it was better either. That's probably why I feel so cross with myself. I feel I've wasted precious time, and missed the opportunity of leveraging my influence and connections in advance of leaving.

Money was basically no object, but here was a charming, talented, urbane man with a history of power, involvement and achievement literally sitting on the benches. He was feeling vigorous and motivated to 'join in' and do something. He just had no idea what that something could be.

Two or three years on

In Henry's case, those two or three years have already elapsed. How do you see his prognosis?

1. **Next steps**
    (a) He continues to wait, doing the same round of leisure pursuits, in the hope that 'something will turn up'.
    (b) Henry talks seriously, at length and often with a group of other men he knows in their later 50s and 60s to see what options he can discover.
    (c) He sets out a framework for himself to prompt possible options: writing a journal, taking a coach, going on a series of workshops aimed at later-career 'reinvention'.
    (d) He slumps further into a sense of isolation and depression.

2. **His relationships**
    (a) His wife feels disappointed and unsettled by the changed dynamics and his negative frame of mind, and their relationship hits a low point.
    (b) The new circumstances cause Henry and his wife to explore new ways to communicate and interact, and provide each other with support to grow and develop as individuals and together.
    (c) He realises that most of his friends have been either work-friends and the relationship flags, or are really his wife's friends and don't have time or inclination for him on his own.
    (d) He uses the situation as an opportunity to deepen old friendships and make new friends.

Now let's take a look at more self-aware, pro-active typologies.

Case Study: The Captain

When I think of the Captain type I see, in my mind's eye, the black and white clips from England's World Cup victory in 1966. Bobby Moore being carried aloft, with the Jules Rimet trophy in his arms. All his troops, dirty, tired and elated around him. But he, Bobby, being the very centre of focus. The Captain.

It's the captain who ultimately says yes or no even to the coach's strategies. And it is the captain who can imbue a game with *fluidity*, responding impeccably to the opposition's tactics, but without deviating from the gameplan. The captain who leads the team out onto the pitch, and the one to whom all eyes turn for reassurance or support in the heat of the game. A good captain knows the strengths and weaknesses of everyone on the team, and has the finely tuned heuristics to play to them accordingly.

Basically, the captain calls the shots. And takes responsibility for winning or losing.

I have found that Captain styles are often in their own businesses, or individuals who have carved their own roles and career paths. Not through 'being asked' or head-hunted, nor even through promotions. But by dint of observing what their passions are, and what strengths they have to make them happen – then having the will, or the energy or the basic confidence to go after them and either ask directly for the role and responsibilities or create it around themselves.

It helps if this has been practiced behaviour over the course of the years. But, as with most behaviours, it can be adopted and learnt at any point if we choose. After all, no team appoints a player to the captain role on their very first game in the sport. They will probably have gone through a number of other positions first, and even have spent some time on the benches.

We might be tempted to assume that great captains take up the role with no dip in self-confidence; that they somehow 'know' how to shoulder that responsibility, in a way that would be totally foreign to the normal player. But according to an interview I read with John Dawes, the victorious British Lions Captain of the early 1970s, his biggest crisis of confidence in his rugby career came when he was given the captaincy. It came almost at the point when he thought he would simply play out the rest of his career as a solid but unremarkable player. Yet by picking up that challenge and focusing on *leading the team* he came to play the best rugby of his life, and realise his dreams of what the game should be about.

I have known Chris for nearly 20 years, and have always admired his style. I don't think he has ever been head-hunted into a role, he has always either gone for it directly himself or built a business around his passion. Besides, I think he is impervious to the Flatter Factor that so many recruiters use to get people to move into roles that actually lead them away from their professed bulls-eye target. (I know all about that. I used to be one myself.) His internal locus of control is so strong it acts rather like a magnetic compass.

It always made me smile that he spent his first few years out of university in the construction industry. Not because his family thought he should, but because they were all doctors and teachers and he wanted to rebel against them instead of conform. But he told me that was the last time he ever bothered with trying to please or upset anyone else except himself about what he did with his life. 'I was so caught up trying to second guess what they <u>wouldn't</u> like that I forgot to think about what <u>I</u> would like! Life's too short for that, even at 26. And it certainly is at 56!'

Over the years he has chosen to move into consulting, first with a global firm then setting up his own business. This was never simply one of those loose-knit groups of occasional associates, but a hand-picked team of movers and shakers with real edge. It gained a huge reputation in its market, punching significantly above its weight. It wasn't always popular either. Certainly not with its competitors, which envied its audacity and new perspectives – but also not always with clients, who sometimes found it just too confronting and in-your-face. But Chris was always content if he could feel it was truly 'authentic'.

Then, just as the business was ramping up, the dot.com boom began and Chris moved into entrepreneurial technology. He figured that he knew his own strengths and weaknesses and that his ability to sum up a situation and strategise succinctly and practically would stand him in good stead. Indeed it did. He became a serial entrepreneur. Many investments worked splendidly, and a number bit the dust. Some he stayed with through good times and bad, some he simply walked away from or passed over at a certain point.

He tells me that some people have chided him for changing jobs and for looking as if he picked up and put down interests. I liked his reply, paraphrasing Bob Dylan: 'I'm passionate in turn about each chorus of the song. O let me live within myself, and stay forever young.'

And what many others did not know, but what I was privy to, was that whilst he devised and stuck to his own gameplan, he was a consummate captain in being able to respond effectively and opportunistically to external events too. In his case I saw in him something of an America's Cup Captain, trimming the sails and tacking in response to the vagaries of the winds and the seas. And always keeping on course.

In his case the winds and seas included a bout of cancer, a very messy divorce and a new baby just around the age when he had previously been planning for early retirement:

Around that point I realized early retirement was not something on my agenda. I'd sort of had it simmering away there as something I would do. But on reflection it looked more like one of those 'auto-pilot' options. The sort of thing you do just to show everyone else you've got enough money not to need to work for the dollars. Similar to my father's generation wanting to have a stay-at-home wife, to show everyone he could afford for her not to have a job.

I feel like I've just got into my stride. There are a whole heap of things I still want to do, and ideas and opportunities to explore. Amassing money and assets, as such, aren't what drive me – but the thought that I'm going to be paying school and Uni fees until I'm in my 70s makes money something I can't just forget either. . . .

In Chris' case his Captain attitude and behaviour is coming to the fore in other ways in the Second Half too. In his previous marriage the arrangement was somewhat more traditional, with almost all of the earning responsibility on his shoulders. This time around he and his partner work closely together on funding their gameplan. Veronica has set up a very successful business manufacturing and selling play equipment. It took a few years for it to gain traction, but now it has clients worldwide and is a solid wealth-producing asset as well as a venture in which they both want to stay hands-on and involved in continuing to develop its reach creatively.

If anything, he's also working smarter rather than harder in this Second Half. The heuristics he has developed seem to allow him to cover more ground with less effort, but greater confidence.

He's also starting to think ahead to later decades and is contemplating retraining later as a teacher. So far he has encountered varying degrees of incredulity and outright ageism in response, as he has started to explore how this might come about. But, given his behaviour to date I'm keen to follow how that intention turns out. . . .

Two or three years on

How do you think Chris' life may be panning out a few years on?

1. **Current activities**
   (a) The portfolio of start-ups and family business will continue to prosper well.
   (b) The portfolio may be patchy and the income irregular.

(c) He and/or his partner may lose interest in their current activities and move on to something else.

(d) There may be some serious reversals of fortune in some of those investments, creating unforeseen financial difficulties.

2. **Future options for beyond the next decade**

(a) Chris will retrain and practise as a teacher.

(b) Ageism may provide obstacles. He may retrain, but will not find active teaching employment.

(c) Ageism may provide obstacles, but he will find creative ways to sidestep them (e.g. set up his own Distance Learning business).

(d) He may find another interest more compelling and go for that instead, related or unrelated to teaching.

Case Study: The Coach

You know the phrase, 'Those who can do, and those who can't teach'. In the sports environment that is sometimes said about coaching. However, although it is true that there are some excellent coaches who have never excelled at their chosen sport themselves, the best and most notable generally seem to have had some high-level competitive expertise too.

Phil Jackson, one of the most successful basketball coaches of all time, had eleven NBA championship rings to his credit: two as a player and the other nine as coach of the Chicago Bulls and the Los Angeles Lakers. Sir Alf Ramsey, Manager of England's first World Cup soccer winning team, won 32 England caps himself. Stan Smith, the US Wimbledon winner and one of the greatest doubles players of all time, went on to set up his own tennis school, the Smith Stearns Academy, and spent time as the USA Olympic tennis coach.

In some ways it ought to sound counterintuitive, particularly in individual sports like tennis or athletics, that highly competitive players would put their own egos and prowess aside to assist others achieve greatness. It's not as if there is the same form of loyalty involved as in doing it for the team in which the coach had his or her own success. Very often coaches join clubs to which they have no prior ties or affections. And nor is it just about the passion of competition, nor solely the thrill of winning.

Mark Henderson, himself an Olympic swim team captain, worked a couple of years in swim coaching after retiring from competitive sport before moving into the finance sector. Yet he still keeps his involvement in mentoring and supporting young athletes today through being Chair of the Athletes' Advisory Council for the US National Olympic Committee. Currently highly successful in international finance, he still says that his dream job would be as a college coach in his own later-career.

That connection is important to him, he says, because:

> I remember how much it meant to me to have someone passionate and experienced to take an interest in *me*. It helped me develop my technical skills in the pool, but more importantly than that it boosted my confidence and my mental abilities to take on the challenges. In my mind, being a coach is as much about helping those new stars be the very best they can be in their own lives and as people, as it is for them to be the very best in the pool.

As a typology the Coach is a contrast to the Captain style as their forte is in extrapolating their own experience and heuristics with the intention of passing it on to others, as opposed to the Captain who is more likely to change the game and explore new areas.

In the world of work, I'm sure we have all had memorable coaches in the form of mentors, either formally or informally. Some individuals are naturals as coaches in this sense, and have the knack of doing it even in their 20s to newcomers to the operations. For others, it takes until they are further along in their own careers before they notice either the urge to offer back their experience to assist others, or feel safe enough in their own position to reach out to up-and-comers rather than feel threatened by them. This is when a sense for Generativity kicks in.

We examined the concept of Generativity in detail in the previous chapter. To recap, it can briefly be explained as an attitude to life which is geared towards improving the lot of those who come after us. It is an approach which goes beyond simply caring about what happens to one's own family and children in the future, and the patronising aspects inherent in traditional philanthropy. So it is intrinsically linked with broader social engagement and the issues of Sustainability. Bob Buford coined the phrase that Generativity represents the transition from '*Success to Significance*' (Buford, 1997), or as Dan P. McAdams calls it, 'the new definition of worldly success' (McAdams, 2001).

Remember also, as explained in Chapter 2, that acting in some form of coaching capacity is only one subset of ways one can manifest Generativity. In that context, now we are looking at the Coach type in particular, I need to put in several *caveats* for the reader.

Coaching, or mentoring, has become the trite default button as the kind of thing one might be expected to turn towards in later-career. Yet the truth of the matter is that not everyone is cut out to be an effective mentor! I have seen a couple of initiatives around this fail miserably, run by large manufacturing and resource organisations in the USA and UK. The simplistic approach they took involved setting up a mentoring system for younger managers, in which the mentors were chosen not on a volunteer or aptitude basis, but simply by being deemed to be in the later stages of their career.

In the same way as not every senior executive is naturally talented at selling, or at giving memorable and entertaining presentations, not every senior executive can be expected to easily make the transition from directing and doing to *advising*. The difference is that if the employer wants them to improve in selling or presentation skills they usually train them. In the case of the mentoring frameworks I am referring to, neither mentor nor mentee was given any training, monitoring or debriefing around skills and expectations. And even if they had been, just as with the other skills, it remains a fact that not everyone turns out to excel in coaching or mentoring, even with some degree of support, and nor do they necessarily enjoy it just because they are in later-career.

One of the younger managers in one of these schemes in the UK, who had been matched with a more experienced mentor, put it particularly pungently. 'I never got the impression his heart was in it. He never seemed to look comfortable when we got together. Funny, I'd always admired him so much from afar, seeing him run the regional accounts. But he was utter shite at passing it on!'

There's a caveat too around Board work, which I see as very much related to the Coach type. My good friend, and for many years my own mentor in Executive Search, David Nosal (of Nosal Partners with its international HQ in the USA), carries out a high number of Board-level searches every year. According to him, a major prerequisite of being a good Non-Executive Director is the ability to tap into your career's heuristics, then distil it into good advice.

'Too many Boards, and too many aspiring Directors make the mistake of thinking that experience and a track record of successful leadership is enough,' he says. 'In practice, some of the best CEOs make the worst Directors because they can't let go of the compulsion to *do* instead of advise. That's not good for them, the Board or the business. Getting on a Board, or several, is still seen as the 'crowning glory' of success in leadership in many quarters. But if I sense the candidates haven't moved into that space I tell them, "What the hell are you looking at Boards for? If you want to continue leading and running the place, go out and set yourself up a business. You'll be far happier, and no doubt far more successful."'

For this example I am going to relate some of my own story. For quite a while now I have specialised in consulting and executive development for later-career executives and their organisations. I have worked with public and private sectors across Europe, the USA and North America. I've always taken an interest in Alumni affairs and have been President of the Cambridge Society and on the Alumni Committee of my MBA School, the Australian Graduate School of Management, but have tended to look at my involvement as an external advisory or fund-raising capacity.

However, several years ago now I was invited by Anne Lonsdale, the Principal of my old college at Cambridge – New Hall – to come to an informal dinner she was organising to help brainstorm ideas for supporting and enhancing the students' confidence and acuity in both entering university life and leaving it. With hindsight I now recognise how clever she was in bringing together a group of us who were all Alumnae 'of a certain age' (that is, in or approaching Second Half), and how her vision resonated with our burgeoning senses of Generativity.

What was created, over the course of the next three years or so, was the Gateway Programme, a ground-breaking off-syllabus set of workshops to augment (or supercharge, as we prefer to describe it) the high level of academic study at Cambridge. First Year students are being coached in practical life/work skills like self-awareness, decision-making, time management and prioritisation implementation. Final Year students are immersed in experiential exercises to help them determine their own values, link them to career targets and understand the connection with business ethics and corporate social responsibility. We also offer one-to-one career-choice coaching. Not in competition in any way to the Careers Service at the University, but as a bridge or encourager to take up the Careers Service's offerings in a more focused, confident and savvy way as a consumer.

Honed over the last two years, we are getting remarkable feedback from students, parents, Directors of Studies and potential employers alike.

From a personal point of view I have found the work utterly absorbing and rewarding, although it has only taken up a minor portion of my schedule. After one full Sunday of hour-long career-coaching sessions I remember emailing a friend to rhapsodise about the pleasure I had felt in seeing the young undergraduates explore, grasp and extrapolate around the career options available to them and go away excited at the prospect of moving ahead with their targeting. Definitely an 'And they pay me for this?!' moment for me.

Because indeed one of the beauties is that the college approached Alumnae first to consult on, and put together, the concept and has established it as a commercial undertaking. Given its success at pilot stage we are now in the process of gaining sponsorship for the Gateway Programme, with particular interest being shown from organisations with a true commitment to diversity. (New Hall is one of only two remaining all-female colleges at Oxford and Cambridge.)

The added, and unexpected, element to this is how the concept has evolved 'organically' into a tailorable programme for other educational establishments. The key elements of business ethics, values-driven career directioning plus understanding the necessity of economic sustainability for individuals, organisations and economies have been found highly attractive to other universities and business schools, particularly in emerging markets. The response has been particularly strong in ex-Communist states, both Eastern Europe and China, where there have been no role models for career choice for at least two generations because the governments moved people at whim. In fact, it has been so positive that I am wondering how much of my time and my focus it, and other similar projects, will assume during the coming year and beyond!

Two or three years on

Given the nature of this new work, and my own situation at exactly 50 myself, what do you see as the range of outcomes I might expect?

1. Focus
(a) The early-career focus will continue as a sideline interest to my main specialisation in later-career executive development.

(b) I will be enjoying the tie up between my career in head-hunting and career directioning for younger leaders so much that it will achieve equal focus within my current business operations.

(c) The thirst for learning and growth from the undergraduates and MBA students in the emerging markets will prove more appealing and lucrative than pushing uphill on executive later-career consulting, and I will put the latter on the back burner.

(d) Both early- and later-career consulting involvements will continue to extend, metamorphose and develop and further related options, as yet unforeseen, will arise.

Case Study: The Olympic Athlete

I am conscious that the majority of typologies I am identifying arise from team sports. This may not suit everyone's mental image-making and, indeed, there is one type I've noted which bears the greatest resemblance to an Olympic athlete, in an individual sport.

I had a fascinating conversation with Dan Veatch, US Swim Team Captain for the Seoul Olympics in 1988, which illustrated the connection for me. It's about the power of envisioning, practice and training, then being utterly conscious of one's actions in every moment of the race. It's also about long-term planning, so as to coincide one's peak with the Games (which may be still several years away), through to second-by-second concentration and utilisation of energy.

As a top-level athlete, clearly envisioning the winning race in advance is now an integral part of the build-up. Imagining it and seeing it in one's imagination as clearly as possible has been proven to have enormous impact on performance. Then comes continual practice. Hours and hours of what looks to outsiders like simply swimming up and down the pool, doing the same strokes, the same turns. But what it is achieving is actually allowing the body itself to memorise and internalise in its own muscles the imprint of doing it right. Add on to that extensive preparative coaching and debriefing by a variety of coaches: attitude, stroke, stamina, nutrition. All in preparation for the big event.

And on that day it all falls into place. Standing on the blocks, the swimmer knows his or her race plan exactly. It is not so much about competition, but about pushing to one's personal best – and thereby winning.

On the blocks the swimmer is not thinking about 'winning', but about how to make the very best dive to start the race. At the turn she or he is concentrating on each millisecond of that turn, not about reaching the finish. They are trained not to look at what anyone else is doing (although Dan contends you can 'feel' it rather than see it), because it could be so tempting to act reactively and break the race plan. To be shaken by the sight of a competitor out in front, and to try to put in a spurt of effort rather than follow the carefully thought out, exquisitely personally tailored plan designed to achieve one's personal best.

At the finish line he says the thought is firstly, 'Did I do my best?' and only then, 'Was my best good enough to win?'

We can find the Olympic Athlete type anywhere. Of all the types I have identified it is perhaps the hardest to pin down to a particular background. The common element is some form of enduring passion or focus. I've seen the style exhibited by entrepreneurs and extreme extroverts who have worn their heart on their sleeve about the interests they aim to pursue in later-career. I've also seen it among the most unexpected, conservative sorts who have been happy to get themselves lined up to put their plans into action, in the quiet way their mothers might have collected Green Shield Stamps for later purchases.

And the preparation certainly isn't always about money. It generally seems to involve some form of training and personal or professional development too. Mostly for the related usefulness of it, but often simply for the sheer pleasure of becoming the best one can be. So the type can also be characterised by an openness to improvement, rather than a defensive ego which considers itself already 'as good as it gets'.

A potential pitfall for the Olympic Athlete individual is to get caught up in minutiae, or become too much of a perfectionist in the planning and preparation process. I've seen visions inhibited or missed simply through the compulsiveness of too much tweaking, so that putting it into *action* is continually pushed further and further out. Sometimes until the aim loses the original purpose and thrill.

I would probably consider it the most purposeful of the types. The one which does whatever it chooses in a quest for meaning, beyond mere personal preference. It may be a long-held ambition, or it may be one recently unearthed or found by serendipity. The point is that in the Second Half this is where the move from Success to Significance comes in their lives. (This concept will be discussed in more detail throughout the book.) And the pleasure is playing the 'game' for the sheer joy of doing it, whether or not the outcome wins awards or prizes. It is the true Olympic ideal.

Terry has had a dream for as long as he can remember. Well, at least since some time in his 30s. It is to run a Healing Centre. It would not be immediately obvious if you knew him. He qualified as a Computer Programmer back in the early days of business technology, and worked his way steadily up through one firm to become the MD in his mid 40s. He is basically a quiet introvert and comes across as very much The Company Man. Mr Suburbia, the epitome of the ladder-style career trajectory. Yet for the last 10 years or so he has been quietly lining up his ducks for when he moves out of his current role.

I've always been keen on physical sports – but I never expected them to lead me to more esoteric areas, and ultimately to Healing. Fortunately I've always been quite attracted to, and disciplined about, getting trained up. As a youngster I taught myself how to ski from reading a book. Then later I got into Tae-Kwando and Karate and spent hours practising the moves. I found it, quite by coincidence, a great way to de-stress from work. At first I attributed that to the release through physical exercise, but gradually came to appreciate the mental, and ultimately spiritual, benefits of Martial Arts. I seem to have become quite a proselytizer about all that, encouraging my staff to do something along those lines, particularly if they seemed unsettled, depressed or under pressure. They still rib me about it.

Then gradually, particularly since I met my second wife, I found myself attracted to and getting involved in activities I felt were related to Martial Arts but went beyond them. I'd never call myself New Age or a SNAG (sic Sensitive New Age Guy), but I have got into things like Reiki, Deep Tissue Massage, Zen Meditation. And, although I never had time to study it myself, my wife and I came across this fantastic homeopathic doctor who did all sorts of marvellous things for our health.

So I found myself gradually starting to think more and more about setting up some sort of Healing Centre once I leave the corporate world. I've got to the point where I can almost see the building and where it will be – although we are still debating whether it should be in Spain or in France! And I'm pretty clear on what sort of things will be on the healing 'menu', and how we'll run it as both a general Healing Centre for those who want to come, and as a Healing Centre for healers themselves. Many of whom work for very little and either don't have the money, or give themselves permission to take the time, to recharge their own batteries through Healing, although they offer it to others.

We have a fund for it. And every time we go away we look for potential sites for it. I'm continually looking for new practices to learn, so I can be involved hands-

on as much or as little as I like. And basically because I get such a kick out of the learning too, I suppose. Nothing wrong with that – although I do recognize that all my life I've wrestled with some notion that if I enjoy something it therefore can't be 'work', and therefore can't be 'right' to do. I think I'm growing out of that, though.

And although I can genuinely say I've enjoyed my job, and working for this company too – I simply can't tell you how much I'm looking forward to the count-down to my move to the Healing Centre!

Two or three years on

Once Terry moves out from his corporate role and starts implementing the dream he's been working towards, what are some of the things that may happen?

1. **The implementation**
   (a) All will go according to plan and Terry will wake up (nearly!) every day with a sense of purpose and fulfilment.
   (b) There will be unforeseen difficulties in the set-up of the operation, and it will have to be reworked substantially.
   (c) Terry will become disillusioned as the execution will not live up to his expectations.
   (d) Making the vision real will open up further possibilities for more visions beyond this one.

Case Study: The Master

Tennis is one game in which former stars sometimes choose to stay playing, even if they are no longer playing at their highest peak and consistency. Billie Jean King only retired from competitive singles at 40 in 1983, having played at the highest levels since she was 17, and winning six Wimbledon Singles titles. She continued playing doubles for a further seven years. More recently, in a game still largely dominated by players in their teens, Martina Navratilova continued competing at Wimbledon until her 50th year. She is one of just three women to have accomplished a career Grand Slam in singles, women's doubles and mixed doubles.

In rugby, the legendary Welsh full-back JPR Williams retired from top-level rugby in 1981 at 32 and had no hesitation in continuing to play at club level until well into his 50s. The English fencer, Richard Oldcorn, represented his country in three Olympic Games and has continued wielding his sabre in Masters' Tournaments into his late 60s.

These are only a handful of the champions who seem happy to continue even though their later performances cannot match those of earlier times. For JPR, in his autobiography *Given the Breaks* (Williams, 2006), he says he had a thirst for sporting competition which was not necessarily dependent on the standard of the game itself, and in addition he enjoyed the camaraderie of the team.

For Richard Oldcorn it was simply enjoying the beauty of the sport, and the infinite opportunities he saw in it for perfection. 'Of course I'm not as fast in my reflexes as I was at my peak. But there are certain things I know I'm better at these days. The anticipation, the ability to read my opponent very quickly. Even certain moves. The point for me is to come away still feeling proud of my performance. Nowadays that doesn't even necessarily mean winning.'

So why do some elite sportspeople step down at the height of their power and achievement, while others thoroughly enjoy continuing with their game even if it means dropping to lower rankings? Some say they do not wish to be remembered by their supporters going 'into decline'. Others cite burnout, and for some it is the anti-climax after fighting their way to the top: 'I've got my 50th cap. So what now?'

I'm sure you can see the immediate parallels with the senior executive ranks. Because of our adherence to the ladder principle in leadership careers, it can be very hard for those at the top of their professions to countenance taking on something which could be perceived as a lesser role. Burn-out or boredom may be valid reasons for stepping out of a game, or profession, completely. Sometimes roles below the peak function may not even be on offer as alternative options, as previous Chief Executives or Managing Directors can be deemed as over-qualified for any other role except the top one. And it is sometimes said, and often true, that other members of the team feel resentful or threatened by the lingering power 'aura' of someone staying on after the top of the ladder.

That may be so. But in my experience it takes a person of considerable courage, self-awareness and confidence in their own skin to continue 'playing their game' in later-career but with a lesser ranking, or in a lower league. Braver still to do it within the company or industry sector in which they reached their peak, as that demands putting aside concerns about 'face', personal ego and the worklife version of 'what will the neighbours think'. Such professionals, who can do that for the selfless love of the game, rather than a need to take any job in order to keep solvent, I have found to be very much in the minority.

Howard's career had seen him move through the ranks and, in the FMCG sector, he had been quite visible. After two high-profile CFO roles in firms which were household names, he was appointed as CEO to a third. In the following three or four years in that position he turned the business round and grew it to be an attractive acquisition target, and when the acquisition came about he was made redundant by mutual agreement.

The package was substantial, and Howard found himself in his mid-50s contemplating early retirement. However, after the few months' break of travelling, playing golf and renovating the seaside weekender, all of which had been planned well in advance, he realised that he was still enamoured of the game and keen to get back into it.

I used to meet a number of individuals in his position, so what I found differentiated him from the others was his willingness to look at any role in which he could 'make a genuine difference', as opposed to focusing only on other CEO or MD positions. I found his humility and open-mindedness extremely refreshing. He was one of the very few business leaders who was self-assured enough to tell me that although he had enjoyed his stint as CEO, and had performed extremely well in it, he had probably enjoyed some of his previous roles more and had often felt more fulfilled and stretched in them. I am certain that there are many others who have the same thought, but feel constrained in admitting it.

He was put up as a CFO candidate for a couple of searches, but the final decision, particularly in one of those instances, suggested that the incumbent CEO felt uncomfortable and possibly threatened by a person with Howard's CV coming in to a key role on his team. I believe he looked at other leadership roles too.

When I came across him around two years later, he was looking energised and in excellent form. He had found his way into the Interim Management field, and was starting his third contract assignment. 'I was slow to be accepted as a viable solution at the start, but word seems to have got round that I get my kicks out of a good turnaround and that I'm not after the full-time job. I don't mind helping anyone else look good. I'm over the need to prove anything, and this set-up gives me just as much thrill and enjoyment – but nowhere near as much stress.'

Two or three years on

What do you think might happen over the next few years for Howard?

1. **Market reaction**
    (a) His reputation as a first-rate interim executive will ensure him continuing fruitful employment for as long as he chooses.
    (b) He encounters increasing ageism against his interim candidacies, as certain potential employers interpret his preference for interim roles as evidence of slowing of faculties, rather than personal choice.
    (c) He finds the allure of running the business from the top still attracts him and he eventually takes up another CEO role through a VC firm's approach.
    (d) He chooses to take longer gaps between assignments and starts to build himself a broader portfolio of interests, both in business and in the community.

***

DEVELOPING THE GAMEPLAN:
Create your own role model

Questions & activities to help you understand yourself, your situation and attitudes and start building a picture of the role model you want to become

1. Identifying with typologies

In this chapter we identified and described the types commonly found confronting their own Second Halves:

- Defender
- Referee
- On the Benches
- Captain
- Coach
- Olympic Athlete
- Master

> In each of the typologies, what were the situations or behaviours with which you identified?
>
> Arising from this, are there aspects you would like to see more of in yourself? And less of?

2. Create your own metaphor

The strength of metaphor is twofold. Firstly, with the minimum of language it offers an image of a concept which is open to layers of interpretation, personal choice of meaning and a complexity or sophistication which goes beyond the words themselves. It can be a useful bridge between the world of fact and logic and that of interpretation and meaning. For example, John

Bunyan's *Pilgrim's Progress* (Bunyan, reissued 1996), with its Slough of Despond and characters such as Mr Worldly-Wiseman and the Giant Despair, and the New Testament parables offer a reader scope for analysis beyond the words on the page. Good children's stories use them all the time to stimulate imagination and new perspectives in their readers.

Secondly, neuro-linguistic programming techniques provide evidence that vivid mental images act as the most effective touchstones, or calibrators, for our behaviour. Indigenous communities consistently use animal totems as a form of metaphor, so that an individual can monitor his or her behaviour against the desired traits of their chosen creature. Two senior executives whom I know and respect highly have chosen animal metaphors for themselves. They use them as calibrators for their actions, as in 'Would an eagle do this?' or 'Would this fit with how a bear would approach the issue?'

The premise of this book is an extended metaphor about how the Second Half of our lives (the years from 50–100) can be as animated, stimulating and successful as the Second Half of a sports match.

What metaphor would you like to choose for your own Second Half?
Captain?
Strong and steady team-mate?
Marathon runner? Etc.

It does not need to be a sporting 'totem'. It could be from Nature or Literature. If that appeals more, what does it look like for you?

What is it about that image which attracts you?
What will it help you calibrate and keep on track about?

What can you do today to be most like the image you have chosen?

4

Winning against the odds
OR
Overcome obstacles

Whenever I mention this step as part of a later-career discussion, most people's first thought is about confronting ageism in society. There certainly is deep-rooted ageism as an external force to contend with. But in many ways the more damaging form of it is the age-prejudice we carry about ourselves, which can form obstacles of our own making.

I always think it is curious to reflect that ageism is the only prejudice which catches up with all of us. Anyone can be anti-women or homophobic in the happy certainty that they will never turn into what they hate, fear and disapprove of. Xenophobes are usually those who travel least, and thus have least likelihood of being discriminated against as foreigners themselves, so they are most likely safe from experiencing the same prejudice against themselves too.

Yet we all grow into the people about whom we once held those ageist preconceptions. And time teaches us the folly of them.

Peter, approaching 60 and newly married with a young son, remembers himself even in his 20s thinking that his mother and stepfather married purely for companionship and couldn't (or wouldn't!) bring himself to believe that they could be having an active sex life 'at that age'. He's certainly lost that ageist misapprehension.

And Elizabeth, with a long and distinguished career in insurance, shame-facedly recalled to me how she had looked at a boss of hers, earlier in her career, who was 62:

> I thought he was putting it on, the enthusiasm and the energy he seemed to put in to the job. I thought it was an act he felt he had to do, because once

he was that age *surely he must just be looking forward to retirement and taking it easy, so why not just stand out of the way right now?* I feel so embarrassed and cross with myself that I made that glib assumption. He was only the age I am now – and I would be mortified if I felt any of my team thought that about me. I'm just getting into my stride and am going at it all full-blast. I don't have to waste time on the positioning or the posturing any more, just the job.

These prejudices are quite entrenched, and very widespread, particularly concerning the capacity or even interest in working longer than the traditional minimum retirement age. I liken the attitudes to those held by many of my father's generation when I was growing up in the early 1960s. I remember a number of 'uncles' who said they failed to understand why a woman would want to go out to work if she had a husband with a decent job. In both cases, the misconception is that 'work' is simply about money, and not interpersonal dynamics and a sense of achievement and belonging.

The good news however, for you as leaders, is that they are like a number of other challenges you will have faced, based on ignorance and misinformation. The arguments or assumptions are refutable by fact, and minimised by identifying them properly and offering alternative slants. As we shall go on to explore in the following chapters, leaders have the opportunity and, I would go as far as to say, the *responsibility* to use their platforms to change such perceptions and remove remaining obstacles to seamless Extended Careers from the course. Not just to earn the goodwill of other individuals in later-career, but to allow the organisation and the wider economy to reap the advantages of a higher ongoing participation rate and to stem the loss of the knowledge base and practiced management experience.

So it is disappointing to see some executives walk away too soon, worried in advance about an ageism in the workplace which they may or may not ever actually meet – and which, with judicious use of their platform of authority and influence, they could actively seek to dismantle.

Worse than that, though, are the Defender typologies who refuse to look at reality and who assert that there is no generic ageism. By this they do not mean that they see no discrimination, but they choose to interpret it as a *personalised* discrimination rather than a discrimination towards *all in that age group*. In fact they are usually quicker than most, to the point of paranoia, to accuse others of not appreciating their worth, of being threatened by their experience and of generally being incapable of sound decision-making about talent.

Confronting prejudices

There are twin dangers inherent in their sort of response. Firstly, it moves the discrimination from something easy to understand because it is objective (as in generic age discrimination) into something highly personalised. And personal criticism or rejection, which appears to be levelled at one just by dint of being John Smith or Jane Brown, undermines one's self-confidence and resilience very quickly indeed which, consequently, tends to cloud one's judgement too.

Secondly, and more importantly, by denying the validity of the discrimination being generically age-associated, it does not allow any party to identify the root issue, address it and solve or minimise it.

The key is, as in sport, to 'Call it like you see it'.

Another aspect of ageism to consider is that it may well be the first, and only, form of discrimination towards themselves that an archetypal WASP *male* executive has ever encountered. If this is the case it can be particularly hard for that person to deal with. It can shake one's view of the world very deeply, especially if it seems to come out of the blue. In its overt cases it can be downright shocking to the system; although it is the covert as opposed to the overt responses which in the longer term can be most frustrating. Those more accustomed to being on the receiving end of harassment or prejudice like blacks, females and those with disabilities or a strong foreign accent, on the other hand, have the jersey, have played the game, have picked up the 'rules' – and by Second Half are adept at preparing themselves to ensure they get the best win out of the situation.

I remember when I first encountered gender discrimination. It was in my first job after graduation, and I was in a rather sought-after graduate trainee role. As a woman I was in a small minority, one of three out of twenty. But I was used to that, because at university there had been a ratio of seven male to every female student. And at university, truth be told, the scarcity value and even tokenism could actually work in women's favour for Club and Society elections, so I had no anxieties as I went out into my first job.

I was totally unprepared for the culture I entered. A few weeks into the role, we were all sent away for an intensive training week. By the end of it, I realised that there were some rumours going around that I was having a fling with one of the other trainees. I found the nastiness of the rumour-mongering and ribbing among the rest of our group was harsher and more hurtful than I had ever experienced before. And I should point out it was confined among the young men, not the other two young women. What perplexed me, as well as unnerved me, was that we all knew the story was totally unfounded but it seemed to take on a life of its own. The majority seemed to *want* to believe it, so they found it convenient to say they did.

It got worse when back in the City. These unfounded, so-called 'funny stories' were shared with others higher in the organisation. I was called in by my Mentor and by the Head of HR and given a thoroughly embarrassing and confidence-draining talking to about the dangers of mixing business with pleasure. And the male I was supposed to have been canoodling with? No talkings to, and a couple of weeks of congratulatory nudge-nudge, wink-wink by other blokes along the corridors who had heard he was 'getting on alright with one of the other grad trainees, ha ha'.

It shook me enormously. I could not believe that so-called adults could be so manifestly unfair.

I recognised the situation when I heard from one very successful executive who had an experience of age prejudice which forced him to change his outlook. He has been a sought-after figure in the creative side of the agency world all his career, working in the USA, Asia, Europe and the UK. In his late 50s, after a couple of years of semi-retirement, James felt the urge to get back into the cut-and-thrust of the business. Money was not an issue. He was open to all sorts of options, from part-time to project work, full-time or advisory as long as he could use his skills and expertise in an interesting way.

His first shock was with the recruiters. He made contact again with several whom he had known for a number of years, and who had courted him on many occasions to move. They all met with him, but after the first meeting he found them quite elusive and vague about opportunities for him. None of the multinational names figured in their conversations, and he was not put forward for any roles.

I started to see the pattern. If it was an MD role, they were looking for someone who 'could grow into it'. If it was some other Top Team role, the story was that I was 'too experienced' and they needed someone more junior. If it was clearly a role which needed my sort of seniority and expertise, it turned into a case of 'wrong culture fit'. I started to bypass the headhunters and go and talk to some of my old contacts within firms themselves. Same story. I began to get quite a complex. Had I blotted my copybook in a way I hadn't realized before I stepped out two and a half years ago? Had the market changed so much that my type of creative, client and management skills had suddenly become redundant? Had I lost my touch, and everyone knew except me?

I don't think anyone was exactly malicious, but there was no way they weren't aware that they were being ageist. Maybe not totally discriminatory, but my age clearly bothered them. I'd been there myself, I knew that too. I'd always said 'The Ad industry is a young industry', and I counted myself as one of the young right up until I semi-retired a couple of years ago.

I still do think of myself as young, in that context. Meaning flexible, having a can-do attitude, a bit of a dynamo. I look around and I see kids in their 20s who are nowhere near as 'young' in the way they work and their attitudes. We'd used the term so . . . imprecisely. It's never been about the age, but the attitude and energy-feel. When I've tried saying that, though, I get the Mandy Rice-Davies look back which says, 'He would say that, wouldn't he'!

After my couple of years break I'd come back on the scene with huge energy and excitement, and a conviction that I'd actually 'got it' about the creative side. And that there was nothing I needed to prove about myself any more, just a desire to do a great job with some great people. I'd got ideas that felt newer and more bleeding edge than anything I'd been involved with before. Yet, with all the knockbacks, I felt my confidence gradually beginning to slide.

The parallels are clear between the discrimination that occurred at the start of my own career and what many males experience in the later stages of their career: unexpected, unfair and hard to know how to respond to.

Tess Finch-Lees is Director of The Global Effectiveness Group, and is an anti-discrimination specialist. The advice she gives is simple and straightforward:

Call it as you see it. It's hard to do when you're very junior. You think you might have misread the signs so are loathe to risk being seen as high-maintenance. Later in your career you'll probably know exactly how to read the signs, but might worry that you'd lose face by challenging it. The thing to remember though is, what have you got to lose? If you're being squeezed because of your age, for example, you won't get the break anyway. If you flag it up, play back the scenario fairly and objectively, that way you get it out in the open. At least it's on the agenda, difficult though that may be. Discrimination, however subtle the manifestation, cannot be addressed without first recognising that it exists. Use your influence to stir up the debate.

It turned out that James worked on that advice. He did play back to the recruiters and his old contacts how he read their ageism. He hopes that by doing that it made the matter more visible to them, and got them to look a little more closely at their preconceptions and examine their validity. What he did had no immediate miraculous effect, he says, inasmuch as neither the recruiters nor old contacts did an about-face and offered him a role they had previously held out on. But through the discomfort they showed at being challenged on the subject, he hopes that he added to the groundswell which will eventually change opinions on later-career. And, rather to his surprise, he found it altered his own take on how he looked at an Extended Career and ultimately gave him greater freedom.

It probably took me reaching the very bottom of the curve before I realized I needed to be looking at the situation as an S-curve. In fact one of a series of S-curves, as I'd remembered from something I'd read by Charles Handy on how we should handle work projects and our careers. Basically, once you see you are almost at the top of an S-curve, you need to find another S-curve to move to – or it slides into decline.

It made me realize I'd been approaching my Second Half as if it was exactly the same as my First Half. Same type of job, same type of company, same hiring approach. So I thought, WHY? I can cry 'unfair' about discrimination, and I seriously think it is harming the very businesses I wanted to help. But it jolted me to reconsider whether I had more options than the knee-jerk ones to which I'd reverted. How else could I do a great job, and with great people?

It took me nearly another year, but I took it into my own hands. With two other friends we set up a small operation. None of us had done anything like that before, and it didn't look like anything we'd ever seen either. Two of us have been in the same field, but the third was in finance and is a technology whiz. We're what I think are beginning to be called 'Olderpreneurs'.

What we've got now are a couple of well remunerated contracts for strategic work in this country, with clients we like and have partnered with for years and that is funding us to do some really exciting, ground-breaking work online. We're setting up a form of accessible, affordable knowledge-transfer on marketing and branding for emerging markets. It's incredibly mind-stretching and rewarding. And the good news is, of course, that I would probably never have had the chance to develop this if I'd have gone back into my comfort zone.

One of the most public demonstrations of ageism recently in the UK was the toppling of Sir Menzies Campbell as leader of the Liberal Democrats at 66. As I heard one journalist from the BBC say, 'With the best will in the world he could never be described as youthful'. It may have been the contrast with the younger Conservative opponent David Cameron, or his pinstriped, 'old-fashioned' demeanour which brought the age issue to the forefront. Rather embarrassingly so, one would have felt, for a party keen to assert its – literally – liberal and socially egalitarian policies and, one would have thought, encourage Extended Careers. Especially as Sir Menzies, or Ming as he was generally known, was seen as one of the strongest all-rounders in terms of national and foreign policy across all the party leaders, active among the electorate and an energetic opponent in the House.

In contrast John Howard, Prime Minister of Australia until November 2007, played his age as an advantage during his final term in the role. He consistently refused to hand over to 'a younger man' in the shape of his Treasurer, Peter Costello. He had come back from the political grave-yard in his 50s himself, returning to the party leadership and then winning three terms in office to become the second longest serving Prime Minister in Australian history. As a long-time Australian resident myself, I have to confess that I never liked the man or his policies, but his attitude to leadership in one's 60s was a plucky and popular stance in the country and set a stirring precedent for those in their Second Half. Of all the reasons that were offered as to why he lost both his seat and the election to Labor for the first time in nearly 12 years, age was considered a very minor factor.

As in the business world, the trend for political leaders seems now to be for them to be younger rather than with grey-haired gravitas. I would be extremely interested to see what surveys of the voting population have to say on this issue. Is it just a fashion within the parties, which means the electorate have very little real choice come election time? And is the fashion attributable to a lag-effect? Tony Blair and Bill Clinton may have appealed to the Baby Boomer masses when they were elected, but as the median age (i.e. most common age) edges closer to somewhere in the 50s one would expect not just a tolerance, but a preference, for political leaders of a similar age group. Or, at the very least, a broader spread of age and experience including the 60s and beyond too.

Myths and realities

It is far more sensible to be clear about some of the unconscious, and some-times conscious, ageism that one may have to tackle in the Second Half. Forewarned is forearmed.

There is a whole raft of misconceptions, prejudices and plain Old Wives Tales about older people, not only in the work environment but in terms of capabilities and disposition in general. Here are some common myths, and the research and reality to explode them:

Myth: **Workers in later-career are less productive**
Reality: **Older workers can be as productive as younger workers**

There is no significant overall difference between the job performance of older and younger workers. Productivity is influenced by a number of factors including, for example, days lost to absence which has been shown to be lower in older workers. Productivity is also linked to engagement and involvement, which is one of the main challenges to maintain in later-career, especially if the individual feels he or she has plateaued and is neither advancing nor learning. According to Forte and Hansvick (1999), laboratory-based research suggests that between the ages of 20 and 70 there is a negligible decline in people's physical and mental ability to perform everyday tasks. Variations *within* an age group far exceed the average differences *between* age groups. In fact, older workers may be able to compensate for any decreases in speed by increases in quality, accuracy, sheer practice or heuristics and their interpersonal communication expertise.

Sometimes lower productivity is blamed on sick leave. If it is assumed that older workers are more fragile and take more sick leave, it gives rise to the fallacy that they are less productive because they are away more often. This assumption is totally unfounded. Over 50s often show lower levels of short-term/non-certified sickness absence than younger workers, which is the biggest source of absence and disruption for employers. On the other hand, older workers sometimes show more long-term/medically certified sickness absence than younger workers, although the chronic diseases thought to lead to long-term absence appear to occur across all age groups indiscriminately.

Related to that, too, is the stress factor. Work-related stress, as a productivity diminisher and health danger, has been increasing over the last two decades. Yet, interestingly enough a University of Michigan study (University of Michigan, 2007) presented at the annual meeting of the Gerontological Society of America in 2007 claims that those in later-career suffer less stress than their younger counterparts. The researchers examined different kinds of job stresses reported by participants between the ages of 53 and 85, and how they related to workers' life satisfaction and physical health. In general it was shown that they reported less work-related stress than those of younger age groups. Only 15% reported that their work often or almost all the time interfered with their personal lives and less than 2% said their personal lives interfered with their work.

Myth: Older workers will retire before the investment in training pays off in the long term

Reality: The term for return on investment in training and development is getting shorter, and younger workers tend to have a higher turnover anyway

All workers, both older and younger, need to upgrade their skills on an ongoing basis to be productive in the rapidly changing knowledge-economy. The investment in sophisticated leadership skill development for enhancing a generative approach (as in Jim Collins' Level 5 leadership) could have an even greater ROI over several years than money spent on a younger worker's technological upskilling, and both are likely to stay with the company for the same amount of time these days. Recent studies strongly indicate that as we get older we are in fact usually better at integrating and assimilating new material into our existing skills and knowledge, through an increased ability to see 'the big picture'.

In addition, the 2006 HSBC report 'The Future of Retirement: What businesses want' (HSBC, 2006) cites statistics that workers under the age of 35 tend to stay only three years with the same company, that 80% of younger employees have been with their current employer for no more than five years and a third have been there for less than one year. In contrast, workers over the age of 50 have been with their employers for an average of 14 years. As Dr Sarah Harper, one of the contributors to the HSBC report, said at one of their workshops in Hong Kong, 'If you train workers in their 40s and 50s you train them for the next 20 years or so they will spend in your organisation. If you train workers in their 20s you may well be training them for your competitors.'

Myth: Older workers are unwilling or unable to adapt to new technologies

Reality: Older workers have the ability to learn new knowledge and keep pace with younger workers

Older workers generally recognise the need for continuous learning – but have the least percentage of training budget spent on them.

Cognitive functions such as mental processes – memory abilities, reasoning, thinking, problem-solving and understanding – are thought to deteriorate with age. However, decline with increasing age is not inevitable. There are vast individual differences in cognitive functions at all ages, and there is some evidence that older workers may be able to prevent or compensate for any decline in these functions. In addition, older adults have some cognitive functions that are more advanced than younger adults and, therefore, have much to offer the currently changing work climate.

One impressive demonstration of willingness and ability to continue learning comes in terms of technological take-up. For example, people over 55 years of age are the fastest growing group of internet users in Australia, and a UK survey of retirees under 75 years found 53% accessed the internet from home.

Myth: Older adults have difficulty adapting to change
Reality: Professionals in later-career may simply be more open, articulate and questioning about change

Often any difficulties perceived may be the result of questioning in *advance*, as opposed to in implementation, and this may occur at any age. Given that senior managers are likely to be more confident in expressing possible misgivings, and that later-career executives will have more experience of previous change programmes which would be useful to acknowledge and share, it is likely that such response could be misinterpreted as being against change when in fact it is about risk minimisation.

One of the conclusions arising from the evidence is that older adults are vastly different from each other. This is as a result of both external and internal factors that interact with the process of ageing and, therefore, no stereotype of older workers is likely to be true for all, or even most, older workers.

Diversity parallels

A number of companies around the world are beginning to look at the issue. However, as with the early stages of most new ways of looking at the world (like other facets of Diversity or Sustainability), there is often more rhetoric

than reality. I saw a programme on British TV in 2005, an episode of Pan-
orama, called 'Must Have Own Teeth'. It was an exposé of the ageism and
entrenched prejudices and assumptions around older workers. It pointed out
that even the organisations ranking among the Top Firms to work with had
less than 10% of their workforce over 50.

All women, particularly in the higher echelons of leadership, know about
living under those sorts of situations of obvious under-representation, produced by deeply etched societal prejudices and behaviours. A UC Davis
study in July 2007, looking at the Top 400 companies based in California,
one of the more advanced States concerning diversity, revealed only 10.4%
of Board positions belong to women. An IONWomen study of February the
same year noted a rise of less than 1% regarding numbers of women on
Boards across eight States of the USA. The second biannual European PWN
BoardWomen monitor 2006, published by the European Professional
Women's Network, had a slightly healthier picture of around and above
20% for female Board members in the Scandinavian countries but only
11.4% in the UK, slightly lower figures in Austria, Germany, France and
the Netherlands. Other EU members with even lower diversity on Boards
were Belgium with 5.8% and Italy with 1.9%.

That last survey, and one published by the US-based research organisation Catalyst in collaboration with the Institute for Management Development in Switzerland earlier in 2007, points to gender stereotyping as one of
the main obstacles to larger numbers. Catalyst's President, Ilene Lang's
opinion is, 'In this increasingly competitive global marketplace where companies must fully leverage all talent, they cannot do so if stereotyping of
women prevails'.

The link between breaking gender stereotyping and ageist stereotyping is
inescapable.

Training and development for the over 50s: an oxymoron?

Over the years I have approached a large number of organisations about how
far their executive development programmes include their executives in
later-career. I've lost count of the times I've heard, 'We don't need anything
like that, we're a very young company'. What they really mean is, 'We want

to portray a "youthful" face to the market, by which we mean flexible, dynamic and energetic'. That attitude then blinds them to the fact that they may have staff *of all ages* with exactly those attributes, so the issues of later-career and Extended Career, along with the benefits that could be accrued, become invisible.

I have heard that line from a very well-respected, diversity-friendly law firm founder in Australia, who was himself in his 60s, with half the team of Practice Leaders well into their 50s. He could not seem to see the mismatch between stereotype and reality. On another occasion I heard from the National CEO of a consulting firm, who was going to retire within the next 12 months, that initiatives around later-career performance development were superfluous. 'We're a very young company,' he told me too.

'But your HR Director tells me that over 28% of your Partners are due to retire within four years.' I countered.

'Ah yes, but we feel we get a far better ROI from training in the much earlier parts of their careers.'

I questioned this too. That 28% of the Partnership group are almost all likely to stay on for all of those four years, possibly even longer. They have amassed expertise, client contacts, a knowledge base, so all the company has to do is support their sense of engagement and purpose within the firm, to ensure that the best keep performing at their best. In contrast, the figures indicate that at the intake level, the turnover rate is less than four years. I would not suggest cutting development for high-potential leaders, but it is a fallacious argument to say it necessarily gives a better ROI, as so much of the investment in junior leaders is actually realised in a competitor's business rather than their own.

Sadly, the adage 'You can't teach an old dog new tricks' is taken far too literally and enthusiastically by most firms as an excuse for not investing in continuing development, honing of skills or, most importantly, the fanning of the flames of motivation and engagement. With less than 10% of the average training budget spent on the over 50s, with probably even less than that devoted to them in the management levels, the picture in most company cultures seems to be that once into the Second Half one is only seen as a cost rather than an asset capable of further increasing its worth.

Dr Pat McCarthy is from the Graduate School of Business at RMIT University. As part of his PhD he wrote on inhibitors to performance in older workers. In his research he found that quite a vicious circle had been created, mitigating against re-energisation and revitalised performance.

Organisations are often loathe to spend any money on training and development for their older, more experienced workers, tending to cite the reason that they have become too stale and disinterested to either be interested or benefit from it.

According to Dr McCarthy, *The problem with that is that what they are really seeing is most likely the staleness of being in the same role, when they have mastered their job and no longer find it challenging. Research has shown that in such situations where stretch, learning and curiosity have ceased anyone, regardless of age, will begin to diminish in levels of engagement, self-esteem and probably performance after 3.5 to 5 years.*

It is not necessarily a problem of that age demographic as individuals, but a systemic one. Many older workers find themselves 'plateaued' like this, and with these feelings, in the later stages of their careers. In fact more than 90% of my Case Study contributors provided evidence that they were subject to organisational or structural plateau. They find they are not included in succession planning because of their age, they aren't given learning opportunities and they miss out on interesting projects.

That shows yet again the flaws of a ladder-style career. Once the highest point that a person is likely to reach seems to have been attained, they are too often left in that position 'for the duration'. Organisations seem to lose

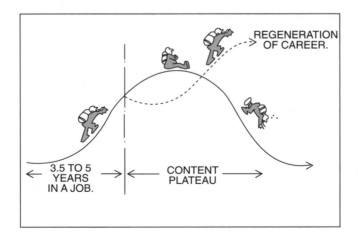

Figure 4.1 Career plateau
Source: Courtesy Dr Patrick McCarthy, RMIT University, 2007

interest in them at that point which is, of course, a tragic paradox. It is likely to be their peak performance period too, yet it can be the time when they receive less notice, support and challenge – which is obviously counterproductive to maintaining that peak performance.

The additional trouble is, as Dr McCarthy points out, that disheartened and disengaged workers (of any age) can be a negative force, resisting change and giving less than their true potential. Unfortunately it still seems that the older the professional, the more likely they are to be set up for failure in this way, because of the system:

> I was surprised by the level of anger I found when I was studying workers in a large organization who felt their careers had stalled. Because we are all working longer, and older people tend to stay in the same jobs for longer, they may be pissed off and under-utilised for 10 years.

Where these plateaus are imposed, leaving people feeling helpless and embittered, both workers and employers suffer. Any business truly committed to sustainability should see the fundamental inconsistency in setting up older workers for failure. The Extended Career cannot expect to pay high-performance dividends if it is stripped of all engagement and enthusiasm motivators. This is most particularly the case if it is contrasting with a more dynamically paced and stimulating earlier career.

I often make the comparison between this situation and how, five years ago, training on Corporate Responsibility or Sustainability was rarely on an organisation's agenda yet today it is. In that comparison, the pressure has been mounting from investors to show solid sustainable policies, and from clients that their suppliers should be good corporate and social citizens. Unfortunately, when there is no overt pressure from such groups in a market-economy sense, corporations continue to see Extended Careers only as a nice-to-have but with no financial imperative. As they become more sophisticated in understanding the component parts of building a truly sustainable organisation, I believe they will realise that the support and encouragement of sustainable, Extended Careers are all part and parcel of that. Without any external pressures, however, it may take as long to self-regulate as achieving gender equality in executive and Board roles. . . .

As I introduced in Chapter 2, I maintain that obstacles and ageism can be overcome far more swiftly when governments exert influence. After all, the support and encouragement of a workforce which works longer in life impacts on individual businesses in one highly beneficial perspective: increased potential for productivity.

For governments, whether UK, US or European, there are two further important perspectives: the shortfall in pension provisions, made more acute the earlier that workers take retirement; and the costs to a health system from basically healthy people in their 60s or 70s who succumb to the well-documented statistics of sickness and decline once they are removed from the active participatory environment, which work constitutes in most cases. If not working they will be less likely to be on private, company-sponsored medical insurance, so the taxpayers will have to foot the bill. Dr McCarthy also points to the link between ill health and people left in roles in which they have become passive rather than engaged.

It is inescapably a government's responsibility, whether liberal or conservative in ideology, to maintain social and economic stability and sustainability. For that reason the challenge of keeping people at work, engaged and productive, is far more urgent and visible on a macro economic level to the government than it is to business, large or small. Although moving towards the concept of longer-term sustainability, business' focus is still shorter-term and parochial, rather than looking at the greater good of the broader socio-economic community. So I support a governmental role to incentivise industry, whether through subsidies or tax breaks, to take on greater responsibility itself in turn.

Anti age-discrimination policies, directed at employers, are part of the solution and are being rolled out quite effectively. Should there be appetite for a truly radical solution, I would recommend similar policies to that which Norway introduced regarding raising the percentage of female Board Directors. In 2003 the government introduced legislation requiring all listed companies in the country to increase female representation on their Boards to 40% within five years, or face delisting or even closure. Of the 487 public limited companies and 175 listed on the Oslo Stock Exchange, less than 25% have failed to comply (to date). Although highly controversial, the result has been to see an increase from 6% of Directors being female in 2001 to 37% by the end of 2007.

'This trend would not have happened without regulation,' said gender equality Minister Manuela Ramin-Osmundsen. 'Business organizations have tried for 20 years to boost the number of women on Boards, but they have been unsuccessful.'

By the same token, why should there not be age-related legislation, either as incentive targets for tax relief or as quotas which would be punishable by delisting or similar sanctions?

Setting policy is one thing. Supporting it through education and action contributes enormously to its proper implementation. I have witnessed this scenario in microcosm within a large corporation. I was called in to a major retail bank for advice about its age-friendly diversity policies. They appeared to be best practice, state-of-the-art policies, openly and fairly offering managers from 55 upwards the full right to rewrite their roles so that the organisation could retain their knowledge and experience. The managers could ask for transfers, part-time, project work, job-sharing or any other option and the company promised to work to make their request happen. They could not understand therefore, when the policies had rated so highly in internal surveys, why their staff were not taking them up on the opportunities.

It was quite simple. Through focus groups and individual, anonymous responses to questionnaires it became apparent that the managers simply did not know what to ask for. Once again, the issue of role models comes into play. Over 60% were quite open about the fact that they had never seen any examples of alternatives to a regular full-time role, except in the form of maternity leave or for mothers with children. They simply could not imagine what other formats their contribution could take, as they had never witnessed any.

This was also the first time in many of their careers, some of which spanned more than 30 years in the same company, that they had been asked about work preferences on any significant scale. It had been the norm for the majority to be promoted or moved by the company, as opposed to applying for a role, so they had no history of making substantial choices or internal applications themselves. The staff at which the policies were aimed had scarcely any previous practice in this sort of decision-making, which we eventually realised accounted for their reticence and lack of confidence in taking up such a good and sensible policy.

Also, the longer the policy was in place but with lower than expected take-up, the more there arose the totally unfounded perception that perhaps the firm didn't want staff reworking their roles in this way after all. That, of course, had to swiftly be nipped in the bud to avoid loss of credibility.

The outcome was that my client realised that these type of policies need more than a launch through publicity. Because they are so new, and are about fundamental change to attitude and action, the people at whom they are targeted need to be prepared to understand and respond. In this case, the preparation took the form of online interactive information on what the variety of options for recutting roles might look like, plus group coaching and workshops. In this way the take-up rate doubled after the first pilot sessions. The process had tilled the ground for the staff to understand why it was introduced and that it was genuine strategy not lip-service; it had shown potential templates for the format of roles and offered space for experiential exploration of options in a safe environment. And it had offered peer-group learning and support regarding how best to approach and then implement these transitions.

The same sort of intervention is necessary at a national level. How is the workforce expected to prepare for Extended Careers when we have never encountered them before? Those who have been entrepreneurs and run their own businesses all their lives are possibly the luckiest in finding the transition easiest. They have a significant amount of practice in exerting control over what they choose to do and when.

It can be far more difficult for those in corporate life, public sector or academia, particularly if they have long tenure in only one or two organisations throughout their previous careers. How do they cope with the ageism within their organisation which they may begin to face, having never been subjected to discrimination in their lives before? How do they find out what the alternatives to the 'ladder' are, and experiment with them as approaches well in advance? Having been unlikely to have had any practical career management advice at any other point in their life, who will assist them with it at possibly the most difficult point of all?

A New Age for education

As I have made clear earlier, the majority of businesses still either see no point, or seem unwilling to pay for such training and support. Compounding the problem, individuals themselves are often in denial that they will need such assistance and/or have never been in the habit of paying for their own training, particularly if it has the feel of 'personal development' as opposed to a hard skill. I have seen even those with plenty of money plan and fund months of travel, but become downright mean about paying for 'some course'. And those who do decide that they would benefit from such assistance, well where do they go?

If individuals and companies will not fund direct methods of equipping those in the Second Half for a meaningful, productive longer-than-they'd-originally-expected game, where else can it fall but to government? If the government recognises the needs to keep its valuable population working longer, to fund their longer lives so that they will not drain the country's financial resources, then this should be viewed as judicious investment, not 'cost'.

I have long lobbied for government-supported preparation for Extended Careers. I see it as education and development, rather than necessarily new skills training. In my experience, in one's Second Half, particularly at the management levels and above, it is not new skills which need to be learnt but new *attitudes*, which lead to new, more functional and beneficial *behaviours*. Above all, it is about permissioning oneself to reframe conditioned views on who and what we should be in the Second Half.

In Figure 4.2, the vertical axis shows the years from 1900 to 2020. The horizontal axis shows chronological ages, in this instance of those being offered formal education. In the early part of the 20th century, the emphasis was on junior schools, keeping children at school only long enough so they could do basic reading and arithmetic. Between the wars more focus was

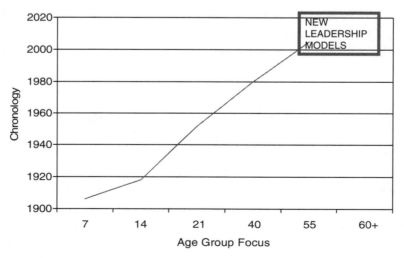

Figure 4.2 Education and training trends

placed on keeping children at school until mid-teens so that they could have a more rounded education touching on history, geography and science, etc. to equip them for a broader set of work opportunities and responsibilities. Around the same time, basic supervisory education for adult workers began to be introduced in some factories and offices.

Following World War II, university education was opened up to far more teens and early 20s, and business schools offering MBAs for graduates in their 20s and early 30s became more widespread. By the 1970s and 1980s management education, in the form of corporate education programmes at business schools, universities and in-house training took education into the sphere of those in their 30s and 40s and older. The fashion for leadership education today covers most age groups from teens upwards.

The only area which now appears to be without purpose-built education is for the Second Half professionals, particularly those moving into later-career and extending their career beyond what would have been the traditional retirement age.

The spread of education upwards through the age range has come about not through warm and fuzzy philanthropy, but through sheer economic pragmatism. Economies began demanding a more sophisticated, better-prepared workforce. Where private industry was demanding a greater number of better-educated specialised personnel, the private sector tended to provide the means such as through MBAs or senior management education. Where the economy as a whole demanded a cleverer, more competitive population government invested, through building more state schools and subsidising university places.

There are government initiatives to help young people find work, get long-term unemployed back into work, and for the disadvantaged to get viable work. So, with the situation being now that our Western economies need to keep workers of all levels working longer, or risk being bankrupted by outflows from pension funds, surely it falls to government to both promote and underwrite moving that line up into the 50s and 60s?

Much of the focus on those forms of programme is on professional skilling, but additionally they tend to have an underpinning of life-skills too, for the obvious reason that they give a context and a 'basecoat' for the practical skills to be painted upon.

My contention is that our later-career leaders, who would otherwise simply retire, do not actually need much reskilling in hands-on work terms.

What will free their potential for generative contribution, engagement and continuing financial reward falls far more into the realms of life-skills, new role-model design and attitudinal, behavioural change. And at the very foundation of that comes '*permissioning*', allowing highly successful executive types to break the habit of the ladder approach to career, which has served them to date but cannot go beyond the top rung. Thus allowing them to step off and envision a Significance which can transcend Success.

Then, as always happens with market forces, once this education becomes mainstream and the norm, private providers will come in to take out some of the government's need for ongoing investment. As the role models for later-career become more attractive, so too will the aspirational nature of further education. I can easily envisage business schools starting up MBAs or practical DBAs in Generative Leadership, aimed at the Baby Boomers. As traditional MBA numbers are dwindling all over the world, why wouldn't they attract the very leaders who took their original MBAs in their 20s and 30s and felt they benefited and were better equipped to step into a new phase?

New MBA formats, such as the Green MBA offered at the Dominican University of California and the Bainbridge Graduate Institute in Washington, are attracting a new clientele. According to Jane Lorand, one of the founders of the Dominican University's programme, it is an audience which would not be interested in the traditional form of Business Masters. Why wouldn't 'olderpreneurs' be an equally hungry market?

Harvard Business School used to run something along those lines with their Odyssey Programme. In the early 1990s, Professor Shoshanna Zuboff founded the executive education programme 'Odyssey: School for the Second Half of Life', which she led for the next 10 years. The programme addressed the issues of transformation and career renewal at midlife, and ran over the course of a year via guided retreats and individual work on oneself.

SAID, the Oxford Business School, has recently introduced a programme in conjunction with Common Purpose, the UK social leadership development organisation called 'What Next?' They describe it, very cleverly, as aiming at 'leaders with more to offer'. It is an intensive five-day programme, with follow-up, for those experienced in leadership positions who are within a few years of leaving, or have recently left, their senior roles and are wondering what they will do next. Their slant is that it is for anyone preferring to put their energy and leadership experience to work in society, rather than just retire from professional life.

In a similar vein, and targeted for a similar audience, my organisation runs five-day Intensive Residentials, with follow-ups, and one-day Introductory Sessions to the concepts in this book. (See www.CGAcademy.org or www.winnersinthesecondhalf.com for full details.) In them we offer a fast-track to the level of self-awareness and guided reflection needed to best visualise what 'winning in the Second Half' looks like to each individual participant. The takeaways are practical tools for self-discovery, which assist in re-engaging with a true sense of meaning and purpose, and build to a solid plan of exploration and action.

In all of the above cases, a number of the participants are financially supported by their organisations. As more later-learning options come on to the scene, I foresee that happening more often, in turn creating a request for tailored in-house programmes, with the funding being taken back by business. This in itself would provoke focus on how to build in preparation for Extended Careers, earlier in the executive development interventions.

Ideally, of course, instead of trying to cram everything into 'emergency surgery' prior to a retirement date, the awareness, concepts and planning actions should be paced throughout the career. I have worked with both law firms and consulting firms on how they could weave preparation into their normal Partner Development programme. For one this took the form of blending into the training at the usual milestones: becoming Partner, mid-career consolidation and Team Leadership responsibilities. For the other we created mixed-age workshops on four leadership catalyst points, so that the subject of age would not be seen to be singled out. These were on the topics of: Managing New Partners, Maternity Leave, Mid-Career Retention and Later-Career Options.

Obstacles of our own creation

So much for the external obstacles, and the external forces of ageism. But before we leave them, it is worth reflecting on the fact that ageism is the only focus for discrimination in which we all eventually become its victims. Look at the stereotypes and assumptions earlier in this chapter. If we believe that a fair percentage of the general public have conscious or unconscious conditioning around what people in their Second Half can or can't, should or shouldn't do, it stands to reason that we may also (still) be carrying around those assumptions in our own heads, unconsciously, even though we have reached that age ourselves.

It is something we should consciously examine, as such thinking patterns become self-limiting beliefs and inhibit our own responses to prejudices against us. They can act like a ball and chain on the ankle of a hurdler, not at all conducive to being able to leap over barriers.

It is important to question oneself at two levels. Firstly, 'How much do I believe that someone in their 60s does not have the energy to run a company/join a new business/be a credible leader?' And secondly. 'Because I am that person now, and I may be prejudiced against myself.'

If there are elements of buying in to those stereotypes, they must be acknowledged and the mental script rewritten or that ball and chain will be clanking around impeding progress for absolutely illogical reasons.

I have known Susannah for many years through the formal and informal networks of senior businesswomen in California. She has been a role model and mentor to others on the issue of gender and racial stereotypes, and ways to overcome those barriers. In her career in the retail and pharmaceutical field she had to rewrite her own conditioning about what she could achieve, as a black woman in business, and has helped countless others do the same for themselves.

Despite her own awareness of stereotypings and the self-limiting beliefs they can induce, she had an 'Aha! moment' one day when her daughter pulled her up on her own attitude:

'Did you hear what you just said, mom?' she asked me, with this expression like I'd said something shocking. 'You said, "I'm too old for that". Mom, I've never heard you say you were too female to do something, or too black. Who *is* it that won't let you this time?' And she was so right. I've always gone right in and confronted the people I saw showing prejudice and old-fashioned chauvinistic ideas. But this one caught me, like I just grew into it. When I reflected on what my daughter said, I realized I couldn't think of anyone who'd stop me going for the project I was after. It was something in *me* saying I was too old.

Of course when I stopped and thought, there's no rational reason for me to think that way. I wondered was I using it as an excuse and that I actually didn't want to take on the challenge about the new programme? That might have been okay – but I thought hard and that wasn't actually the case.

So you know what I did? I flagged it up with my coach. The firm believes in coaching and I've had one for over five years, and we get together at least every month. He helps me to spot when I'm making ageist assumptions that could impact on my performance, and to see when I'm making it my new excuse instead of getting to the real problem.

The process has also got me thinking forwards too. I'm 57 and I haven't put much thought into what my next five years will look like, let alone the next 10 or 15. I've been on auto-pilot for a few years I reckon. I may just carry on like I am, I may not want to, or the company may not want me to. I've got my finances and investments sorted out pretty well. But it doesn't seem very sensible not to spend a bit of time mapping out what my options are, and what I may still have in me to do that I haven't done yet.

There is another side of the coin to watch for, particularly as a leader. It is, 'How much do I believe these stereotypes for *other* older people . . . just not about myself?' Fine, if you can say unequivocally that you are not shackled by limiting preconceptions in your own life. But if the blinkers come back on again regarding anyone else of a certain age, then you could be perpetuating the cycle, which is a waste of your own leadership platform and influence as a change-agent and misses the opportunity for helping others in a similar situation. If you are consciously or unconsciously setting yourself up as 'the exception to the rule', you may still come across the ageism of others who lump you into the same basket regardless, and find yourself without the satisfaction of a support framework to counter-argue the fundamental misconceptions about Second Half performance.

Two other internally produced obstacles to exercising one's leadership in the Second Half are grief and fear. There are grief and fear attached to any transition, and the discomfort that change brings. It doesn't have to be due to a sudden bereavement or a single event like a later-career redundancy or retirement. They can creep up on one gradually, almost unnoticed, until one day there is the realisation that there is no going back to the safety zone of 'how it was before'.

Let me draw a comparison with women's experiences again. Menopausal women know that although their fertility has been declining throughout their 40s it is only once their menstruation ceases that they will, definitively, be unable to have further children. Or any children at all. As with all major life events, it is not a simple black or white reaction. I can tell you there is often a sense of relief that one needs no contraception any more, and will escape the tedium of monthly periods. But there is also a grief for the children which might have been, but now never will be. The fear that if one of the major reasons for being here, procreation, is finished there will be no 'real' meaning or value to one's life any more. There can be a fear of losing one's usefulness and even sense of self; and grief over opportunities one never took. At some point there is acceptance that that is just how things are, and that life is subtly but inescapably changed. A chapter closed. It takes longer for some to reach that point than for others.

As William Bridges says so encouragingly in *The Way of Transition* (Bridges, 2001), 'Change can happen at any point, but transition comes along when one chapter of your life is over and another is waiting in the wings to make its entrance'. At that point, it is not about denying the importance of one's life and expectations to date, nor feeling that they have somehow been invalid all along. It's simply about letting go, and finding out what is on the next page.

Of course that is not always easy. Change and transitions often have a habit of sneaking up on us, and demand a letting go quite a while before we feel comfortable doing so. And with that, totally naturally, comes grief and fear.

During my head-hunting career I would hear grief and fear regularly in interviews with candidates who felt they had plateaued in their careers, in the same way that Dr Pat McCarthy from RMIT University did in his researches. Twenty-odd years of being groomed as a high-potential executive, then a dawning realisation that this was as far as they would ever get, certainly within the company and probably even if they tried their luck elsewhere in the field. The knowledge was painful that they no longer figured in the succession plan, except regarding who would take their place. With the ladder as the only valid career trajectory in mind, it can be a shock to the system that the top rung of the ladder now, realistically, will never be reached. It doesn't have a place even in a pipedream. Of course if the ladder is the only model one has ever used as a template, it is no wonder that the emotions stirred up by plateauing, or 'reaching one's peak', can be powerful and confronting.

'I didn't know whether I'm angry, jealous, outraged or what, seeing what I think of as these young muppets being given plum projects which I know I could deal with better. All youth and brashness, but I wouldn't call any of them a safe pair of hands.' This was one of the reactions I heard from a very successful funds manager who was clearly grappling with the grief and bewilderment around a sense of 'changing of the guard – before I'm ready'.

As all grief counsellors and psychologists will tell you, grief and fear are best acknowledged and processed if one is to progress. What people often get confused about here is that the grieving does not necessarily have to be undertaken in isolation, as in separating oneself from the world to go through it. It can perfectly well be defined and processed concurrently with other normal, gainful activities. Or it can be given space and time. Both approaches segue way neatly and obviously into a solid base from which to draw that next S-curve, write the next chapter or start a completely new volume.

Certainly some people find it preferable to take time out, take a sabbatical, set up a period of semi-retirement or, as it is often termed in the USA, take a 'first-retirement'. Those drained by symptoms of burn-out and leaders and executives who have been concentrating almost 24/7 on work-related concerns, as opposed to their personal concerns, may well feel they need such a break and some space in their lives to regain perspective.

A word of warning though. This is best approached as part of the Extended Career plan, not like emergency surgery. Particularly for those in the Defender mould, the effect will be far more beneficial if a time-out period does not have to coincide with panic at a retirement or redundancy point.

It also needs full understanding by the person that although they may *desire* a quick-fix or 'solution' to the unease they may be feeling about what the Second Half may bring, this is one time in life where it is imperative to delve within oneself, find one's own style of play and not abdicate the responsibility and opportunity by taking on something prescribed by someone else. In those cases it may only compound the sadness and fear in the grieving process, and even delay moving to the next stage. That may well take some time.

The good news is, of course, that by this stage one has far more innate ability, heuristics and good sense gained from the years of life experience to be able to make those decisions oneself, than one had when the first and earlier life and career decisions had to be made.

Those who do have the idea of an approaching transition already in their minds are much more likely, and more able, to benefit from contemplating any grief and fear as part of their normal life regime. I tend to find that women are much better at this than men. As Gail Sheehy expresses in her work *New Passages: Mapping your life across time* (Sheehy, 1996), women's lives, particularly for those with children, are far more attuned to identifying and coping with life transition and change points than are men's. In my own workshops, when we run exercises around Transition Points or Re-Invention Points, I nearly always find women can identify, codify and articulate their transition points far more intuitively and analytically than men. This seems to equip them better to prepare for the next ones.

Women also tend to do support groups so much better too. They get practice through the physical-change aspects which men do not have to negotiate: antenatal groups, mothers' groups, menopausal groups, etc. Women also gravitate towards AA (Alcoholics Anonymous), post-prison support and disease/trauma-survivor support groups in far higher percentages than their male counterparts. If organised religion can be construed as a support group, women also make up by far the largest percentage attending Christian churches. The taboo about seeking help and support does not exist to the same extent in female society, nor the shame or pejorative implications in having sought it, as it does in most male groupings.

Women are also far more likely to create informal support networks around specific issues than men, not just through close friends but with work colleagues and even strangers who share an interest area. I find it particularly interesting that there are a plethora of women's networks and women's fora in organisations as diverse as the ABC in Australia, to IBM globally, to Hewlett Packard in the USA and Marks & Spencer in the UK. Some are actively incentivised by the company, others emerge spontaneously.

Yet there are very few networks for individuals, of either or mixed genders, who are in their Second Half and/or approaching transition beyond their career to date. Some excellent ones are gradually appearing on the internet, such as www.aarp.org in the USA and www.maturetimes.org.uk in the UK. Their appeal is due, no doubt in large extent, to the 'privacy' aspect. They are virtual, and interaction can be totally anonymous. Why is that, I wonder? Mainly because of the taboo which still surrounds the subject of later-leadership.

The age taboo

There is still a very strong taboo around discussing age and daring to explore what is beyond the traditional career and retirement scenario. I have been called in a number of times by companies because they said they wanted to discuss issues around later-career and transition among their management staff, but who very quickly talked themselves into believing that there was no problem at all *because the older management staff did not agree that there was any*.

The fact of the matter was that those in leadership who called us in were absolutely right. Their gut reaction about performance, engagement and anxiety about the future among their older senior team members was absolutely correct. Yet it was seen as weakness in individuals in their later-career to admit to anything that was not 100% 24/7 commitment and focus on the job in hand, so the company culture was perpetuating the taboo and strangling the exploration of how to keep these good guys longer and performing more productively and happily.

This taboo can become very pronounced towards a distinct 'retirement'. For the leader right at the top, and those at any level of authority and power, there can be a concern about becoming like a 'lame duck President'. In the case of a President it is the fear that, once it is known that there is only a short run-up to the next election, their power base will evaporate and transfer allegiance to whoever looks as if they will take on the mantle next. At the tactical level it's a fear that however compelling their mission may be, and their strength to accomplish it, they may end up sabotaged by others preferring to tread water and wait to see what the next incumbent will do instead.

At the emotional level it can be anxiety that one is perceived to be dropping off into the retirement abyss. With the paucity of appealing role models for that, it is not always something one wants to admit to, especially if an A-type and someone used to being admired and envied. The individual is even less likely to want to be drawn into discussion about 'afterwards' if he or she has no fixed plan of action. Again, it can be very daunting to find oneself without a twelve-month, two-year or five-year plan for the first time since leaving university. It can lead to a downward spiral of denial, procrastination and diminished confidence and poor health.

This is a particularly crucial period for leaders. As the RMIT University research and the Whitehall II Study of 2004 show, an unhappy period in the run-up to a retirement or to a significant later-career work/lifestyle change can mean an unhappy, even unhealthy, period straight afterwards (Whitehall II, 2004).

The final obstacle: What comes next?

Finally, one of the most important obstacles to overcome is a lack of clarity about what could come next. This is at the heart of the stress that the On the Benches type feels about approaching the end of the traditional, pre-mapped career. They have worked so hard as the epitome of the company man, or the family man that they have forgotten what they actually want for themselves.

There are all sorts of books written for 'women who give too much', or who are too selfless for their own good and put everyone else's needs above their own. But there are precious few about the men who support a family's expensive lifestyle by working all hours, seven days a week for decades, tied to the treadmill and feeling unable to either get off or to ask for a less punishing treadmill. There has been very little for the men whose main, but far too infrequent, pleasure is to spend time with their kids and who look forward to some far-off day when they can spend as much time with them as they want; and who find themselves in their 50s and 60s with more time on their hands, but their sons and daughters caught up in treadmills of their own. So what will they do with themselves?

When I meet these types, I have a mental image of someone at the top of a tall empty tower looking down into it. It is as if they have built this impressive edifice with the bricks of their behaviour, building it up brick by brick to become what they think the company or the family wants, until it is so high that they can't see the real person at the base of it, down in the darkness. Not much light is ever allowed to be shone into there, as the concentration is on how the tower looks from outside.

The Referee type also struggles with this. He (for it is most usually a male) is quite definite about what people like him *don't* do in the normal run of things, but is all at sea when there are no rules or tried and tested practices or indeed role models. It is a paradox that often the executives who have looked the safest and most stable during their careers, because they have had security of tenure, a vast underpinning of company infrastructure and a strong company culture to which to conform, turn out to be those who feel the most fragile and disoriented afterwards.

The amount one has to adapt should never be underestimated when having to take up running one's own diary, having no team to which to delegate tasks – and find that all the money is coming direct from one's own bank account and not an expense account!

It is totally understandable that anyone used to infrastructure and highly defined 'rules of engagement' and clear promotion paths might flounder when all that is taken away. As Peter, a Partner at a leading global consulting firm confessed to me, 'For 35 years you have to go where the firm sends you, do whatever it wants you to do, keep within the boundaries and ensure you don't put the company at risk at all. Then, all of a sudden, off you go with a decent enough pension – and are expected to turn into some sort of spontaneous super-adaptable entrepreneur overnight, managing your own new career. It just doesn't happen as easily as that, once all that's been trained out of us by then anyway!'

The Defender style, too, grapples with a different aspect of clarity. In his, or her, case there can often be clarity ('going on a Board or two'), but of a very blinkered kind. It may not be a textbook definition, but in my opinion true clarity is achieved only when a range of possibilities have been explored and analysed. In Socrates' words, 'The unexamined life is not worth living'.

To evaluate those possibilities properly in the first place, there needs to be clarity in the form of self-knowledge – which is what the Defender tends to avoid and cast as 'soft stuff'. In the next chapters we look at how seeking one's significance and leveraging one's platform can help increase a sense of clarity about what comes in the Second Half.

***

DEVELOPING THE GAMEPLAN:
Overcome obstacles

Questions & activities to help you uncover the attitudes and self-limiting beliefs you may be carrying, and decide how you want to cope with the internal and external obstacles you may have to face

---

1. Overcoming external obstacles

It is generally accepted that there is still age-discrimination, of varying levels, in our society and work environments. Some feel they suffer from it more than others.

Do you currently feel any age-prejudice directed towards you?
If so, how does it manifest itself?
What impact, if any, does it have on you?

Have you ever been on the receiving end of discrimination before?
If so, what were the circumstances?
Do you see any parallels with the situation now?
How did you deal with it?
What did you learn from the experience? What worked and what
    didn't?

Have you ever been guilty of any forms of active prejudice yourself?
What were the circumstances?
What was the effect?
Can you think of any responses from those who felt the effect of it which
    might have changed your behaviour and attitude?

2. Tackling self-created obstacles

In all situations we bring certain assumptions and learned behaviours conditioned by our experiences to date. Unless we are fully conscious of them we can tend to carry the same ones around, unquestioned, long after they have outlived their usefulness or validity.

As children we learnt that we shouldn't pick up matches or sharp knives. As adults, or even as independent adolescents, we need to change those assumptions if we are ever to cook on a gas stove! We can identify them as the knee-jerk, 'gut' reactions which surface when certain images or 'buttons' are pressed. If we fail to spot them, and continue to let them direct our behaviour unconsciously, they turn into self-limiting beliefs, obstructing opportunity, happiness and performance.

What does a person of 50 look like? Of 60? Of 70? Of 80? Beyond?

How much do the images which come to mind match today's reality?

What observations can you make about your thought processes in conjuring up those images?

What do you think about life and careers for people in their 50s? Their 60s? Their 70s? Their 80s? Beyond?

Where do those ideas come from for you?

Are you happy that they reflect your real feelings?

How do you think the thoughts above impact, consciously or unconsciously, on your assumptions about yourself in your own Second Half?

Are there any negative preconceptions about age and Second Half you feel you are grappling with?

If so, how does it/they impact on your behaviour and self-confidence?

What self-check mechanisms can you put in place to recognise what prompts them and when they occur?

How do you find it best to get over them?

5

Playing your own game
OR
Seek your own significance

Great players create their own signature style in their sports. They have the ability to transcend the basics of their innate talents and the coaching they receive and to weave them into something new and unique. Examples like Pele, Roger Federer, Tiger Woods, Muhammad Ali all developed an inimitable approach to their field. They play their own game, learning from others yet never giving up their authentic, highly individual style.

Think of the kicking style of Johnny Wilkinson, the two-handed backhands of Chris Evert and Bjorn Borg, the Fosbury Flop. Through their exceptional successes they literally changed the face of the game, leaving a legacy which was of a significance beyond mere personal success. Great players leave a legacy: some consciously, some unconsciously, by playing their own game.

How would I describe the difference between Success and Significance? The ascension from the adult developmental phase of Career/Life Consolidation to Generativity. Success is a personal, more 'I' or 'it' achievement. 'Significance' is both of that *plus* the 'we'. Significance transcends *and* incorporates Success.

The same can be seen among leaders in business or the community, whether we look at President Clinton, Bill Gates, Henry Ford or Nelson Mandela. There are certain people who approach what they do with a generative attitude even before their Second Halves, using their personal goals and values as their calibrators, even though they may not always be accepted or acknowledged by the majority. They play their own game. Far from running out of steam as the end of their mandate comes closer, the more they set their sights on ensuring lasting, *significant* achievements. They do it not for personal aggrandisement, but for the benefit of their team, the field they love, their business or the greater community.

So how can we as leaders, having achieved some success in our First Halves and claiming our Generativity, seek the step beyond – Significance? The key to that lies in ensuring that we are playing our own game, and are in touch with our own inner 'real' self and sense of meaning, not someone else's.

To do that we need to examine:
• Who and what has brought us to where and who we are now.
• How we are who we are now.
• Who and what will make us who and what we choose to be.

Earlier role models and expectations

Throughout the previous chapters we have looked at the importance of role models, and the lack of them regarding later-career today. Now it is time to look back at the role models which influenced our early assumptions about life and career, and started shaping us into who we are today. Through my work in career directioning I see how our theories about life and career are established largely through early role models: at home through the family, by expectations we perceive at university and in the formative first days at work.

For instance: how many of us can trace our choice of school subjects to family influence? Choices which consequently influenced our choice of university degree and perhaps even the university itself. Or were the decisions simply by force of arbitrary circumstance?

I've often posed these questions to people. One very creative-minded friend said he ended up in biochemistry at university because Arts subjects clashed with Science on the school timetable, so he had to cut off his options on a wider spread of subjects aged 16. Another always wanted to be an actor but, typically, put it aside because his parents deeply disapproved. I slightly hesitate to mention an example like that one, in case it sounds overly archetypal and almost corny. What swayed me was his assertion 30 years on, even with hindsight and understanding the concerns of parents first-hand himself, that he genuinely feels he would have made a good and successful actor. My husband confesses that his interest in IT was spurred purely because he thought his sister's boyfriend at the time was extremely cool – and was taking one of the early classes in computing in the 1960s.

I am certainly not saying that such choices are wrong choices, nor choices which blight one's life. External influencers shape one's life very potently in one's teens and 20s, and people still end up happily. At that stage in life more perceptive, reasoned and carefully explored decisions are the exception rather than the norm.

What I *am* advocating is that, around and beyond the half-way stage of life it is far more within one's capability to question these influences and take decisions consciously from one's own, internal locus of control.

Let us examine the likely early influences more closely. How many of our parents, brought up in an era of depression and/or war, inculcated us with the importance of having a safe, well-paid job? In my own case, whilst struggling with a disastrous first job choice after graduation, my parents genuinely thought they were cheering me up and supporting me by saying, 'You can't expect to enjoy your work, you know, especially if you want to be successful'.

As advice for dealing with short-term pressure within a longer-term strategy, it has a lot going for it. In contrast, as a mindset which equates WORK = UNPLEASANT it is toxic. It leads to the misplaced corollary *if you are enjoying yourself it clearly isn't proper work. And if you enjoy your work you should not expect to earn a lot of money for it.* I used to find it fascinating how often these beliefs surfaced when talking to the candidates I used to interview. It accounted for a lot of the internal friction and sense of misalignment that they often grappled with about their careers.

Sadly I still find it cropping up among undergraduates and MBA students with whom I work now. I do my very best to dispel that misplaced belief as soon as possible, as it skews their decision-making process about the roles they target for after graduation.

I firmly believe that it is everyone's right and, when talking of highly educated people, that it is tantamount to their existential duty to both enjoy work and to expect to earn a decent reward for doing and enjoying it!

As an aside, I believe this latter fallacy about 'enjoyable work = lower-paid work' is partly responsible for the demise of teaching and nursing as professions. Due to the excuse that both professions get their satisfaction from the work and not the money, pay and support in both spheres has plummeted over the last three generations until it is now so low that conditions and morale have deteriorated to the point that it is neither satisfying nor adequately paid.

There is also the bind in which many top students find themselves. I call it the Dux syndrome. One colleague, years ago on my MBA programme, typified this. Martin had been Dux (academic top student) of his school. At the start of the course I remember he told me he had been keen to take a Liberal Arts degree of some form but found himself propelled into Medicine:

> I think I got caught up in the worry of having to go from a big fish in a small pool to somewhere I'd just be a little fish again. I felt a pressure to do Medicine. You needed to have got the highest marks even to consider it. So I ended up doing it not because I wanted to do Medicine at all – but because I was worried that other people wouldn't have known I'd been Dux if I'd taken something Artsy. I think that's what my parents felt too.

He did not particularly enjoy the study aspect or the content of the course, but hung on because he thought that all the fuss and encouragement he'd received about Medicine must mean that life would somehow magically get better when he was actually able to go into practice. Within only a couple of years after he qualified Martin realised he was still unhappy, unfulfilled and overworked as a new doctor too. He simply wasn't cut out for it, and his heart wasn't in it. When I met him at the start of that first term I felt really sorry for him, having put all that effort into qualifying for something with which he felt so out of synch.

So he came on the full-time MBA with the avowed intention of radically changing his direction and finding something closer to his own personal preferences. He was a brilliant student and rarely got less than High Distinctions. His greatest interest and enthusiasm appeared to be in HR-related subjects and Marketing. Yet Martin made no attempt to look for openings in those areas as he got towards graduation. I saw him focusing on the recruitment presentations given by the leading Strategy Consultants and he ended up with a couple of well-paid offers.

Why, I wondered? 'I knew I could do it! They only take the best from the A-Team.' I felt far less sorry for him this time around. It sounded so similar to his situation in making the Dux–Medicine link, and here he was doing the same thing all over again. I wasn't surprised to hear later that he had stuck it out for only two years. Anyone with an ounce of objectivity could see that his personality and his preferences would be a highly uncomfortable fit with what he had chosen – seemingly predominantly so he could demonstrate that he had been part of the A-Team at business school.

The question it begged was who exactly was he wanting to demonstrate that to? Having told me quite perceptively why he had made a bad choice in Medicine it would be illogical for him to assert that he was proving something to himself this time around. It's amazing how often people come out with that glib, knee-jerk rejoinder, 'I needed to prove something to myself'. A few moments of introspection and it is highly likely that the person to whom it seems to *matter* to prove something is not themselves at all – and may indeed even be long dead. It is probably the figure of their mother, father, teacher, boss-who-sacked-them or more supposedly successful friends. What liberation conscious awareness of that can confer!

It is hardly surprising these issues occur, though. Career or work–life balance issues are very rarely directly addressed or taught in our schools. Career Advisors do a laudable job, but sadly they still tend to be hampered by a very low reputation. A rather cruel summation of that is the jibe, 'If you can't Do, Teach. If you can't Teach, become a Careers Advisor.' My theory though is that it is not necessarily a failing on their part as professionals or advisors, but a systemic one. The problem is that they are rarely seen as part of the curriculum and 'real' school, so their importance and impact is severely diluted.

At university, for the undergraduate, study for the degree and attaining good marks are focused upon so myopically that there is surprisingly little attention paid to linking the process with *what comes after*. In business schools students pay tens of thousands of dollars, pounds, euros, etc. to take the course – for the fundamental purpose of improving their career prospects and career trajectory. Yet in Britain and Europe the word 'career', let alone any useful content about how to direct it, rarely if ever appears on the syllabus. And if it is not on the syllabus, just as top models won't get out of bed for less than $20,000, so it is that the most competitive and A-type students tend not to bother themselves with anything unless there is a mark attached.

From what I have seen at British, European and US universities, it is gradually changing for the better these days, stimulated by increased competition in the graduate job market. In order to continue to attract the best students, colleges need to have a strong record in graduate placement, so are beginning to be innovative about how they do that. As I mentioned earlier, I am working on just such a programme with my old college at Cambridge, New Hall. I was also invited to co-design and write a new Personal Development module for the MBA programme at The Henley Management College, which we believe is the first time a British business school has put the subject of directioning one's career actually on the syllabus.

The situation was rather different for anyone graduating before the mid-1980s. For most of us now going into our Second Halves, our experience was one of full employment for graduates. We knew there was a job for us after we graduated so, for all the wrong reasons, and peculiarly counter-intuitively, it made many of us less choosy and less curious about what we went into. Looking back, knowing what I know about work psychology now, the attitude was amazingly laissez-faire. 'Let's do whatever this is for now, and we can always change later.'

That is not always a bad motto, but as many Audit Partners, lawyers and bankers whom I have interviewed know, getting off once on a particular industry treadmill is not as easy as it looks before stepping on it. And the pace of life and incumbent responsibilities of family in one's 20s and 30s are not at all conducive to going back to basics at a later date. By that stage it can feel just too hard and time-consuming to work out where else one's passions and true calling might lie, and so much conspires to keep us in harness.

It is very sad, and a sore waste of potential, that so few of us bothered to think critically about what we really wanted to do with our lives after we left university. Very few people I have talked to in my work spent any appreciable time as undergraduates exploring what their motivators, key strengths and potential skills were in order to match them with future careers. Indeed, statistics suggest that we all spend more time per year planning our holidays than we ever do planning our careers.

Maybe there are a lucky few who arrive at Half-Time confidently asserting that they 'always knew' they would be an Investment Banker or Professional Services Partner. But, quaintly enough in those situations, it seems to run in the family or at least through family friends.

Through work I am doing with Cambridge undergraduates at the moment I am rediscovering some other quaint, misplaced assumptions. These include,

'The big banks seem to be the only ones hiring' and 'Consulting must be *the* area to get into as they spend so much on getting the right people'. Yes, even young Oxbridge economists still need to have it pointed out to them that it's only the bigger, richer companies which can actually afford to do the Milk Round to gather up Final Year students, and there are actually lots of other equally enthralling jobs around, particularly if you are willing to be pro-active and make an approach yourself.

However, I don't bring all this up in order that we should be hard on ourselves. I simply want to call attention to the self-awareness *vacuum*, and highly externally influenced environment, in which most of us made our early career decisions. These were decisions which have shaped our working lives. But what else could we have been expected to do? At the time there was no support structure to enable us to do that particularly effectively, and we simply didn't know what we didn't know. Self-awareness was not part of the curriculum, nor part of our work vocabulary following that for most of us. It ran far more simplistically along the lines of mathematicians and scientists become actuaries and technologists; modern linguists and historians go into marketing or HR; and the A-Team and Union Society President types go into finance or the media.

To illustrate, let me recount how embarrassingly truncated my own process of decision-making was about career choice at graduation. I had read Spanish and Italian and I considered myself a leading light in a number of the political and debating societies. The strongest preference in my mind was to go to work for BBC World Service Radio. That was actually quite a sound choice, looking back. I could have used my languages, my natural curiosity about people and issues, and my general interest in communication. And I remember being extremely pro-active about lining up interviews and meetings with senior staff there, with the aim of employment. All fine up to that point.

It was only when I was told, quite charmingly by one of the Directors, that BBC World Service Radio were not going to hire any graduates that year, that the lack of any sensible plan B became glaringly evident. As a somewhat misguided response I rejected the idea of looking into television instead. I really can't remember why and, looking back, I certainly can't have been looking in the right areas for advice! Did I sit down and brainstorm what other opportunities there might be related to what appealed to me about BBC World Service Radio? No. Did I extrapolate upon my own skills and preferences in order to come up with a spread of alternative options? No. I jumped straight on to the young persons' safety blanket: 'What have my friends done, and are happy at?'

The answer, in four out of the five cases I looked at, was investment banking. I did not understand back then that one year's excitement at living in London, and earning rather a lot of money for the first time, did not necessarily mean my friends were happy and in the right job. It was an extended honeymoon period as three out of those four showed, by leaving within the next couple of years.

And even less did I understand at the time that, just because we were friends and had been involved in some of the same activities while at university, it did not automatically mean we had the same skill sets or life preferences. Numeracy, for example, is something I have never counted as anything except something I could barely scrape by on. I said, even then, that I didn't like numbers. Perhaps I could claim that I hadn't really had much cause to practise it up to that point, so I had no idea how much I could really come to hate and loathe Balance Sheets, P&Ls and spreadsheets. The only good thing to come out of the banking experience was that I single-handedly changed the way that particular bank recruited for graduate trainees. They began testing for numeracy.

I was reminded of this when talking to the Olympic athletes I interviewed. They each recounted that when their sports careers were ending and they were applying for jobs, they religiously noted that their major attributes were tenacity, competitiveness, focus and similar things; all the motherhood statements about sports champions you could think of. Every single one of them. As if the whole US Olympic swim team, for example, might be so interchangeable that they could all do as well as each other on any given role – and presumably be equally fulfilled. Is that likely? A very superficial attempt at self-awareness, we decided. If that is as far as it goes, it is a very blunt instrument. As we used to say in Executive Search, once you've got the basics it's the differentiators which create the fit and the magic.

So the challenge I throw out is, do we still restrict ourselves like this 30 years on, when by all objective expectations one should be far more rigorous and sophisticated? Half-Time would seem to be a good time to review and take stock.

If we could wave a magic wand, go back in time and offer advice and support to our young selves about to embark upon a career and a new and unknown stage of life . . . wouldn't we leap at the chance to do it? And wouldn't we want to ensure that we took advantage of aspects of our network or college or Careers Service which, at the time, we did not know existed or failed to appreciate?

I know I would, and that I would have benefited professionally and confidence-wise. And if that support could be organised into some sort of framework, and put on the curriculum perhaps, it would be even more powerful and valuable. Everyone would stand to gain from helping the young players develop their most perceptive gameplan: the college through enhanced reputation for support of fulfilment and potential, future employers in avoiding the waste of misguided hires and the loss of potentially great hires who would otherwise have been blinkered to the opportunity, and the individual in making more effective choices through knowledge and exploration. And it wouldn't be a case of hit or miss that some individuals gained the advantage of timely support and others did not.

So the question is, what stops us from doing the same for a similar big step and new career/life phase: the Second Half? Instead of being armed with just our degree, we are coming out into a new phase with far more to offer – but maybe just as little idea as to what to do with it as when we left university.

Like at graduation it is a point in life where we need to make choices about a future of which we have very little understanding, only this time we have fewer role models. And, again, we don't really know what we don't know. Are we going to take whatever turns up? Or can we fine-tune our self-awareness, explore a wider territory than in our early-career days and script a gameplan which is far more individually, personally attuned than we could have been capable of before?

Who do we become?

Our own Half-Time very often coincides with reaching the top of the ladder. I have met a lot of people who reach the top of the title-tree as CEO or Director. It can be enormously exhilarating. It can be energising. It can also create further expectations of oneself. So much so that the momentum often carries into looking for another, even larger, CEO role, then another after that. And for some, although powerfully energised, there can still come that little thought in the middle of the night: 'Is that all there is?'

It is a truism these days to say that one of the main dangers confronting successful people is identifying themselves too much with their jobs, to the point that they subjugate or lose sight of the 'real' person they are. One way this can happen is by morphing into Company Man. That is, gradually taking on the behaviours 'expected' for success: by following the internal role models within a company culture; by becoming like the successful ones, in the hope you will be successful like them. Cultures each have a 'successful person' mould. One can choose how much to fit or defy the mould, but without a doubt the most comfortable road to success and acceptance is to fit as snugly as possible. It is rarely a case of stark compromise of values, or major ethical misalignment. More often it is in the form of a gradual series of smaller trade-offs, where the change of course can really only be seen properly a long way down the line.

By that time John *is* the Head of a major multinational, as opposed to seeing himself as John, father of Amanda, husband of Elisa, friend of a handful of close, smart people and with a panoply of external interests and passions, with an enquiring nature, a spiritual side and views and opinions across the board *who also runs a major multinational.*

If you think that is over-exaggerating, just ask the spouses. In the UK today the over-50s are the fastest growing sector to seek divorces, despite the fact that the divorce rate is at its lowest levels for nearly 30 years (www. maturetimes.co.uk, 2008). And this is probably the most common cause of midlife divorce. Contrary to what many believe, the majority of such divorces are not caused by the guy in the Porsche running off with a younger model, but a wife or partner saying, 'I just don't know who you are any more'.

On the way up the ladder it can be very tempting to take on the persona of what one feels a successful person should look like, generically. To take on the trappings: the Boxster, the second house in the country, the skiing holidays. And to match the behaviours: ostentatiously confident, workaholic, driven, competitive. The pressures to conform to a 24/7 leadership lifestyle can be punishing.

Sharon Jackson, of Carlton CSR and my colleague in our work at Cambridge recounts that a consistent feature of the senior leaders' retreats that she ran on Corporate Social Responsibility in the Tasmanian Wilderness, was seeing the effect on the executives of gruelling days of trekking, staying in unlit, unheated huts and being totally isolated from phones or other distractions:

> It didn't surprise me that the jolt into such basic conditions made the majority reflect ruefully on the real worth of all their luxurious assets at home. What surprised me far more was that the aspect which had those same men and women literally in tears was their own work–life balance and the recognition in many cases that the trade-offs and monetary success had not resulted in happiness, but an emptiness through a sense of having given their real selves away.

As I have been writing this book I've had a lot of interest from friends, colleagues and acquaintances around the subject of 'portfolio' careers. Many seemed to assume that I would be going into detail about what the likes of Allan Leighton, John Parker and Lord Adair Turner in the UK have been doing, and how they set it all up.

I admire those men greatly, and certainly Allan Leighton's overt enthusiasm for 'going plural' has helped change executive perceptions about work as more than an ON-OFF button. In addition, coming in to those portfolios of activity during their 40s, rather than later, they have helped make diversity and concurrent variety of roles look 'sexier', and something totally viable as a prime of life pro-active choice rather than a move which signals failure to gain full-time employment. They have raised portfolio careers to an almost Gordon Gekko, "Diverse is good" level.

However, there are several drawbacks in focusing on such people and their choices as models. Firstly, they still tend to perpetuate the Ladder model: two Chairmanships trump one CEO role any day. Secondly, their pre-portfolio work put them in the very highest percentiles of global executives, thus enabling them to have a smorgasbord of Director options from which to choose. Those options will simply not be available to all but a very select few and, I contend, may therefore set up unrealistic, and ultimately self-confidence sapping, expectations for the majority.

I can see the argument that Board roles offer great opportunity to practise Generativity. But I still contend there is scope for far more inventiveness and creative risk as a 'portfolio' career for later-career executives than a box full of Directorships.

In fact I came across one example of an ex City Investment banker which I feel exemplifies far more originality and inventiveness. Today, he lives in Devon and is a cabinet-maker, a rare-breed pig-farmer and a business adviser. 'None of the jobs I do relate to each other. I have no background in farming,' he says. 'It would be difficult to find another person with such an odd range of jobs. But I'm more satisfied in my career than ever. I enjoy greater security since I haven't placed all my eggs in the proverbial basket.'

When working out what 'one's own game' really is, the earlier examples may be aspirational – but I believe the Devon man is more inspirational.

Significance takes different forms

The questions which assail many successful people as they approach or find themselves in the Second Half tend to include: So who am I now I have reached the top of the ladder and survey the scene? What do I do when I have ticked off everything on the list for success in terms of money, personal achievement and power? What do I do next? Where's the meaning any more?

It is not only those in the Second Half who can reach this point. Andy Freire was a young man in Argentina who made a fortune in online office equipment during the dot.com boom. By 30 he had made the money, done the deals, run the organisation and scaled the peaks of the commercial world that many twice his age never quite reach. Having pretty much achieved all he had ever seen role-modelled, he encountered the existential conundrum. 'Where is my purpose now?' His search took him into the realm of helping other firms find true purpose for themselves and their individual workers. And, through a chance meeting with fellow-Argentine Fred Kofman, he lent his business acumen to the theme of Conscious Business and 'creating value through values', becoming CEO of the consulting firm Axialent. Andy found Generative leadership relatively early in his career. And in his case, to all who know him, he certainly personifies how Significance both includes and transcends Success.

Several other leaders in their fields, all in their Second Halves, had similar insights. Lance Moir has a unique career trajectory moving from almost child-prodigy in the finance field, to academia and now back as 2IC in a listed high tech business. He believes the trick is the self-awareness always to see oneself as separate from the job or, more specifically, the role itself:

> Work is what I spend my time doing, not who I am. It's the component parts of what I do that are important, not the job itself. For the first time in my life I'm making my own career. In my case it's a repackaging, a 'recreating' opportunity. In the past, well I really hadn't articulated what I wanted or even what I was bringing to any role except the tools to do the job. I was on 'success auto-pilot'. I just got on with things and got promoted.
>
> Now I can honestly say I've got more insight into who I am, I don't have to prove anything any more. I've actively chosen to take on a role which is all about building a business, in size and performance. And doing that is genuinely meaningful for me. It gives me stimulation, enjoyment and the energy, of a sort which is quite distinct from rest or leisure.

Someone from a very different background is Steve Connard, who has worked all over the world as a film script writer and animation director.

Steve had a transition period of career and lifestyle which lasted around four years in his late 50s. At the start of it he thought it would be plain sailing, as he had been a freelancer all his working life and was used to an irregular work routine as well as stretches without work at all. Title and management power had never been important to him. However, he recounts that he found, very much to his surprise, that he slumped very quickly into a depression:

> I hadn't been prepared for it at all. I thought it was only the corporate types who got so involved with their jobs that they couldn't cope with being without them. At first, even when I sat down to do some writing, even for my own pleasure, I'd start thinking, 'I'm no-one any more', and my confidence really suffered. I worried that I'd lose my edge, and I missed being out of the mainstream.
>
> There were ways I could get around that, I knew that. We still have lots of friends in the film industry. And it really means a lot, I think, to most people, to know they're good at something. 'Mastery', I call it. But I've seen a lot of people give up on that, and end up feeling useless once they've given up their long-term career. Their self-confidence and pleasure in life plummets. I was on the verge of that, I know.
>
> Probably what really upset me most was the sense of loss of youth, and the vigour and power that goes with that. I hate all the images which are around about getting older and, worst of all, about 'retirement'. Grey hair, and staggering around and being useless. Because I see myself as being as youthful and sharp as ever. It was an uncomfortable period in getting my head around the apparent contradictions. My partner was still working too, and in the same

field, so that exacerbated the depression and isolation I felt. I hadn't thought about that aspect either.

What helped me most were two things: counselling and sport. The counselling really helped me through it. I could either stay miserable and sorry for myself, or come to an acceptance on my own terms. What came out of it was an understanding that what I was missing from my kind of work was *self-expression* – and still *being good at something*.

So, gradually, I've started building up new outlets for that, replacing the stimulation I used to get out of my career. I've taken up learning languages, which I'd only ever done as a task before, like when I had to learn Dutch to work in the country when we moved there for a while years ago. This time I'm finding it a pleasure and an exhilaration rather than a chore, learning French, Spanish and Italian.

I've completed my Masters in Fine Arts over these last few years. I've had the time to study black comedy, my area of special interest, which I'd always wanted to get into more deeply. I've enjoyed lecturing on film at college too, which is something I'd never even have thought of before. And, best of all, I'm finding that my writing is better, more intense and actually more prolific than it used to be. It pleases *me* more, somehow, today. And I'm still earning money for it, which is what I worried I wouldn't be able to do. I've got a film script on the go, and a number of stories.

And, thinking about the whole youth conundrum, what has actually had a rejuvenating effect on me is tennis. I was a really good tennis player in my teens, but I gave it up as my career took up more time and space in my life. I've taken it up again really seriously, and I'm thrilled with knowing I'm still really good at it. I've had a few elbow problems, but it gives me a real kick to be playing in competitions. Winning too! Doing that and going to the gym have put me in way better shape, mentally and physically, than I was just a few years ago. The body doesn't function as well, just left to its own devices, as it does when one is younger, so it needs to be kept fit some way.

So, now I've come through the down-phase of the transition, I'd say that the most important things to me in my life now are fitness, through sport and gym, and my relationship. I'm much happier in myself as a person than when it was all based on career and *external* drivers and influences. The key, I've found, is that I had to develop a sense of personal worth beyond just my job.

For Steve, Significance centres on 'mastery'. His attitude has much in common with the satisfaction that the most accomplished artisans and artists felt in our pre-Industrial society – the sheer joy of perfecting a craft or a skill. His Generativity expresses itself through his new perspectives on relationship and self-expression, in which ego is replaced by a much more inclusive sense of achievement.

Sea change and significance

In the course of my research I heard a lot about the trend for Second-Halfers to opt for a sea change and move to a different part of the country or overseas. It can be a great way to reinvent oneself, or escape a sense of stereotyping which might hamper the way one wishes to develop, or simply to add a burst of excitement and adventure to one's life. Some nay sayers worry that high expectations may be disappointed, and that the sea-changers will miss their friends and support networks.

Those are certainly risks to note but, at least anecdotally, I have tended to find that those who choose to move in their Second Half, particularly when well into it, are so motivated to create a fresh start that they are more pro-active than ever before in seeking out new friends, contacts and interests. The fact that they are also likely to feel less constrained by the weight of a 'what would the neighbours say' mentality also contributes to them being able to build new support structures which can actually be more practical than those which had grown up willy-nilly where they had had a long-term base.

My parents made a sea change themselves. When my father retired, and my mother was only two weeks short of her 70th birthday, they emigrated from the UK to Australia. In the course of more than 15 years now they have created a far more robust, and fun, support network and friendship group than I remember them having where I grew up. They have transformed themselves before my very eyes from a very quiet, rather risk-averse suburban couple into laid-back, gregarious emigrants. I have no doubt they have added years to their life in the process, and a lot more liveliness to that life too.

However, the phenomenon that intrigues me is a subset of sea change, concerning returning to one's original community. I've now come across what seems like a growing number of Second-Halfers whose sense of Generativity urges them back towards where they grew up. One example I know well is Gerhard Rumpff, a German by birth, who has spent most of his working life running technology companies in other countries, most recently in Asia and the USA. He and his Irish wife Joy, whom he met and married in Australia, have recently moved back to Germany.

In many ways he feels he's done his sea change, or sea changes, already:

I've lived in a whole number of new places. I've enjoyed going in with no 'baggage', no expectations on me. That initial anonymity gives one a great sense of freedom. Now, over the last few years, I've felt a pull to come back to Europe. We put out the intention to be able to come back here to work and, as it turned out, the MD opportunity came up in Germany too.

I'm very conscious of how I'm far keener to involve myself with issues, political and social, and with the community than when I was here at the start of my career. It's like I was focusing on the 'me' in my 40s and 50s, around my spirituality and my family. I'm 60 this year and I see the future as giving something back to others.

Somehow I feel I've got more opportunity, and more drive to do that back here. I seem to feel drawn back to where I grew up, to try to give something back to those who are growing up here now. I'm not totally sure yet what form that will take, but I know it will be in a more active and externalized way than to date.

I'm into my Second Half now, and I've an eye on the final whistle, so I'm committed to really *living* this half. I've a chance now to do something using all the skills and experience I've gained, and I don't want to miss it. To me it's *more* important, and more exciting in that way, than my First Half because there's no extra half, and no replay! I ask myself, were the last 40 years of adulthood what I want to have on my tombstone? What was it worth?

I'm actually excited about focusing on my next ten years. I see it as a perfect opportunity for transformation. How do I convert my compassion and energy into something useful? What is my part to play? I can contribute money-wise to causes I believe in, to make a difference, but I know it will be by playing an active part and taking myself out of my steady work comfort zone that I can keep growing – and really living.

And at present Gerhard is active in two main areas. He has an offer from a local German organisation to move into partnership in a completely new field of enterprise, and he is also in the exploration and planning stages of establishing an international School of Governance to combat corruption and increase administrative effectiveness in developing countries.

Another example is Dan Dumitrescu, who left Romania as a refugee from the Ceaucescu regime in 1981. Since then he has run one of Australia's largest technology businesses, been a Partner in some of the leading global executive search firms in Asia and the USA, and is now back in Europe running a listed software company:

I've been wanting to return to Europe for a few years now. It feels like home, even though we don't actually have a place of our own here yet. We're not sure where we'll eventually settle. Probably not in Romania, but it *is* very important to me that we have some links with it, and are physically closer to it. It feels rather like in Paolo Coelho's lovely book *The Alchemist*. We often have to go all round the world, seeking treasure and enlightenment, only to find it right on our doorstep, exactly where it always was, but that we had to come back older and wiser to notice it is there.

The search for community is mirrored in Mike Butcher's story. At 58, with a series of highly successful Managing Director and international CEO roles under his belt, the dilemma was complex. Mike was born in the UK, had spent most of his career in Australia and had come to consider it home, but he had been living and working for the last nearly 10 years in Hong Kong. When he came to the point of thinking he had carried out his last full-time CEO role, he found the transition complicated by the sense of dislocation at finding himself in a country he had no wish to stay in. Not only did Mike have to struggle with the question of *what* to do, but *where* to do it too.

For those who have ever taken an overseas posting, particularly for promotion, you will readily understand how difficult it can be to re-enter the home country market. If you have come from a relatively small market like Australia, there is not always the range of similarly interesting roles available on return. And often the saying 'Out of sight, out of mind' comes into play, with local candidates being seen as the safer option. So for Mike, he found himself having to weigh up a variety of options; not the least of which being how to balance trade-offs between tax effectiveness and sense of home and community.

He did the usual things that successful executives can do, and travelled widely, sailed to exotic locations and spent more time looking inwardly at himself than he had ever found opportunity to before. It forced him to pick up an old discipline which he believed he had been avoiding for the last few years:

> I used to be in the habit of writing myself a major essay every few years to distil and refine my intentions, what I will aim for, what I want to change, what I want to maintain. It's my thoughts, my observations and, eventually, my conclusions. They often take quite a while to write and are a mixture of bullet points, one-liners, discursive notes and caveats. I write it utterly and totally for myself. No-one else gets to read it. It's just for me. Yet, interestingly, it's not all about me. It's often the focus on what I can do for others which gives me my greatest sense of purpose, and my best understanding of what actually motivates me and gets me out of bed in the mornings.

It seems to be even more true of this latest essay. I perhaps wonder why I didn't get round to writing it earlier this time. Maybe I subconsciously worried that it wouldn't 'work' outside the normal work situation? Anyway, I called this one 'The way forward after 3 years of "retirement"', and I can say without a doubt that it has given me a new sense of purpose.

The unexpected insight it has given me is that the nomadic life I was leading for most of my years as a CEO, and even for the last three since then, was no good for creating what I have been yearning for and looking forward to. I never seemed to have time to follow up with friends and contacts previously, because I was always in transit to somewhere else. I've worked out I want a sense of community, friends, purpose and stability.

I've every confidence that 'community' will come to me, if I put in the effort to come to *it*. You could say I've got a new sense of connectivity. And I've the time now to commit to all those other things I want. I'd describe myself as an 8/10 in terms of life satisfaction after doing that essay, as opposed to 5/10 last year. And, yes, I will continue with working but the emphasis is more on what I can give and the personal interest I have in it, rather than what it can give me. And I don't put business above family any more.

Speaking to Mike, it is clear that he recognises his priorities have changed over the last several years and that his own desires around achievement have changed too. He is happy to embrace the term Generativity, and finds himself particularly drawn to an increasing sense of community and commitment to something meaningful *beyond* business. Yet he makes the point very strongly that it is a timing and personal growth subject too:

My priorities were different back in my 30s, that's for sure. I worked hard and put business first. And I wouldn't change that. That was right for then. This is now.

What all of these examples have most noticeably in common is that they had purposely and actively taken steps to increase their own self-awareness. This has ranged from mainstream executive development modules on their leadership styles and behaviours to voice work through singing or counselling and to more esoteric explorations of their personal motivations and values including meditation, DeMartini techniques and spiritual retreats.

According to Gerhard Rumpff, working on one's personal development has always brought the highest dividends:

The most impactful business training I've ever had was the kind of thing which worked at the very personal level first and foremost. That's the only thing that can genuinely change attitudes and behaviours. Then it's easy to extrapolate on to a business scenario. It's missing the point to think you can do it any other way.

It taught me how to question. It taught me to be continually conscious of the restrictive mental models we carry about with us. The mental models we still have about age and ageing are particularly constricting. I'm very grateful that I was exposed to that sort of leadership training in my 40s. I was a bit skeptical about it at first, defensive. But it opened up doors to me, and created an attitude to life I'm not sure I would have found otherwise.

Silver linings and golden handshakes

There are also a lot of managers who have wanted to become CEO but have topped out at the number Two role or head of a functional specialty like CFO or HRD. Maybe they have missed out on a promotion, or had an external hire brought in above them. The psychology of how they look at what comes next will be subtly different to those in previous examples. How do they make sense of topping out yet still feel energised and committed?

The situation can be particularly disappointing for good 'company' types. One highly respected, and now very happy, senior US executive called Dick spent over 30 years with the same firm steadily and successfully climbing the ladder. Throughout his career he was at the head of the High Potentials list internally, and in his late 40s and early 50s felt confident he was being groomed to take on the top job. This confidence was severely shaken when the Board put out a search for the new CEO, when the existing CEO retired unexpectedly through ill health. When he was eventually told that an external candidate had got the job he admitted that a whole number of thoughts passed through his mind.

The one which shocked him most was the first one which occurred to him: 'What will everyone think?' He was taken aback to find that other people's perceptions mattered that much to him, causing it to be his first reaction. And surprised that, as he tested out other concerns such as, 'Will I be asked to leave?', 'What are the financial implications?' and 'What else can I do?', none of them gave him such a lurching feeling in the pit of his stomach as the reputation facet.

That realisation led Dick to examine his whole attitude in choosing how to react. He became conscious of some internalised script that ran, 'Runners up do the decent thing and leave'. But instead of taking that at face value he thought long and hard. He looked discreetly at other options externally, and talked with his wife and other close friends and colleagues with an openness and frankness he feels he would not have managed before. Dick unequivocally considers that this not only assisted him enormously in his stay-or-go decision, but allowed him to look at the broader issues of Second Half and what he wanted to do with his life and talents:

> If I hadn't had that jolt, and simply moved ahead with the traditional last rung of the ladder, I may have slid later into retirement without ever questioning what I was doing, what I wanted and where real meaning lay for me.

Finally at 54, and knowing and respecting the new incoming CEO, he decided he could make more impact and achieve more of his personal goals by staying where he was. He was transparent with the new leader, acknowledging his initial disappointment but pledging his loyalty and commitment. A sensible and empathetic move, as it is not always easy for a new incumbent to deal with working with other previously shortlisted candidates without such an understanding.

To his relief, Dick also found that his performance and commitment remained at peak levels as he stayed on – yet he somehow found the time and space for other activities which mattered to him, which had seemed to elude him before:

> I'd seen the same thing happen with other friends and colleagues after a serious illness. Thank God I didn't have to learn it that way. It's amazing how we can find 'time' when a jolt to the system makes us realign our priorities.

And he found time to exercise Generativity. For Dick this meant involvement in pro bono work. He chose less fashionable concerns like a black university and Third World agriculture, rather than the Arts or United Way. He started his involvement as an extra-curricular activity, but became intrigued to realise that he had a platform in his profession which went beyond basic charitable giving and philanthropic Board work. He was able to connect and integrate his own involvement through actively influencing his company to engage with these causes too. It became for both him and his corporation an illustration of practical Social Responsibility and engagement, as opposed to something that would have been dismissed as 'grandfatherly charity work' by others in the company – and himself in earlier days.

What if I don't know what I want to do?

A fundamental question concerning our Second Half is: 'What do I still want to do before the game draws to a close?' Curiously, and to many people's own surprise, it can be a very hard one to answer.

Nearly everyone finds the exercise in Chapter 1, about looking at their life line and estimating how long they still have left, both exhilarating and daunting. It can be quite confronting to try to look ahead that far.

Many of the most successful executives have framed their planning around the Quarterly Results for so long that anything beyond a 12-month timespan can make them feel quite uncomfortable. Others are completely out of practice, having put off that type of self-examination for many years, always citing lack of time and alternative priorities. Some have a conditioned reflex, or self-limiting belief, which tells them such self-focusing is selfish.

Or in others' cases if it is 'just' about their own desires and interests they hope it will work itself out with the minimum of input – which is in totally illogical contrast to the work world which requires full attention and ability to plot and steer a distinct course.

It happens that 'What if I don't know what I want to do?' is very regularly the central dilemma which brings participants to the programmes I run, or is uncovered in in-house sessions. It is far more common than most would suppose. So common in fact that it is exactly why it propelled me to write this book and specialise in the transformational aspects of later-career leadership.

The key to finding that out is in allowing oneself 'permission', through giving time and seriousness to the search, to discover some of those desires and interests which may be long buried, unaccountably repressed or previously dismissed as unrealistic or impractical. It's fabulous finding out what can surface; although, of course, it is not always a comfortable process.

The Referee types will continually try to close off options before genuinely exploring them. They will say things like, 'People like me don't do voluntary work/retrain as horticulturists/take up psychotherapy, etc.' But it would be closer to the truth to say that they are probably just in fear of failure. Some are afraid of what they may find and that they may open up a Pandora's Box and end up feeling more frustrated and unsettled than before.

As one very prominent academic confessed to me recently, in the month after he retired, 'I don't know if I want to look too closely. What happens if I end up realizing that I've been on the wrong track for the last 40 years, and it has all been a waste of time? I couldn't face it.' Whilst that sort of response shows a charming degree of modesty and self-effacement, it can also be used as a convenient excuse to avoid valuable, often long-postponed, self-reflection.

Indeed getting started isn't always as easy as it sounds. This is ground which is likely to open up perspectives on spirituality, one's mission and meaning in life, perhaps the need to confront prior failures and disappointments. It's actually the last thing that the average 'successful executive' is likely to have the practice or the vocabulary to articulate – at least without some empathetic facilitation or framework.

In the Developing the Gameplan section I suggest a variety of ways you could choose to begin exploring what you really want to do and be and accomplish in the Second Half. Some are more like introductions to the process, like the '50-4-50: doing 50 special things'. The intention is that they will perk your interest and confidence to delve more deeply for the *motivators*, which will ultimately lead you to the *What* of what Significance will mean to you.

Other recommendations like Mind Mapping, Senssoma, Passion Mapping (See the Developing the Gameplan section at the end of this Chapter) and undertaking other more intensive and experiential self-analysis are there to help you expand your boundaries and explore more broadly and deeply than you are likely to have had chance (or dared?) to do until this point. People often want to know of examples concerning what others have chosen to do in their Second Halves – again illustrating the thirst for role models.

PORTFOLIO MAN
CFO → Board / Stock Market /
   Consulting / Writing

DOWN-SHIFTER
Strategy Partner → Ad hoc
   Projects with prior employer

PRIME TIMER
Law Partner → P/T Corporate
   Partnerships Director at
   major NFP

FINANCIAL FREEDOM
Advertising Executive →
   Independent Financial
   Advisor

INTERIM EXPERT
Finance Director → Interim
   Executive

Figure 5.1 Extended Career examples 1

ENTREPRENEUR
3 IBM - ers → IT start-up
directors

SEACHANGE
Hedge Fund Manager → B & B
owner in Spain

LEARNER/TEACHER
Consultant/Entrepreneur →
Maths Teacher

CSR
Marketing Dir → Buying
Manager for Homeless
Hostels

PAYING HOBBY
MD → Commissioned open-
area play modules

Figure 5.2 **Extended Career examples 2**

There is a beautiful bittersweet poem that most women-of-a-certain-age identify with: 'Warning – when I am an old woman, I shall wear purple', by Jenny Joseph (Joseph, 1997). In it the author looks forward to the time when she will throw caution to the wind, wear clothes which don't match and do things which she enjoyed doing in her youth, but gave up in order to be a sensible 'grown up'.

After all, if you are in your Second Half you deserve to be a little eccentric and try new things. You may not consider it a time to take more risks with what you do, but it is definitely a time to take more risks with who you are. If you embrace the concept of Generativity it frees you up to explore some of the activities you may previously have perceived as 'softer subjects' – perhaps counselling, perhaps a contemplative retreat, some full-on personal development workshops?

One self-exploration activity which is becoming more and more popular as a celebration for one of the Second Half Big-O birthdays is to walk The Camino of Santiago. This is the mediaeval pilgrimage route from the south of France to the tomb of Santiago in North West Spain in Santiago de Compostela. The whole walk is nearly 800 km, or nearly 500 miles. To walk the whole Camino takes between 25 and 40 days, depending on one's speed and inclination, although a very large number choose to walk only sections of it at a time. The appeal seems to lie in that it is both a physical and a mental/spiritual adventure. Covering largely mountainous and wild terrain (with the need to cross a few high-speed motorways too), it is physically rigorous and demanding. And unlike a safari or adventure holiday, it is usually done alone, with accommodation in rather primitive pilgrim lodges and plenty of time to reflect on one's past, present and future. All of that offers an experience unlike the average 'Work hard, play hard' vacation.

In previous centuries in our own societies there were more rituals to mark transition from one stage of life to another. Of course they still exist in more so-called primitive communities. They provide periods or events to allow contemplation, feel societal support and encouragement, and generally ease the discomforts and fears of change. Like today's baptisms, Bar Mitzvahs, weddings, etc. the aim is to offer a space through which to pass and emerge as the 'new' you – not rejecting, but including and transcending all that went before.

Permissioning oneself to set intentions

Transition periods, when there is a sense of belonging no longer to the past yet not quite to the future, can be very unsettling times. Much seems so fluid that it can sometimes seem hardly worth the effort to make any plans or set up anything to look forward to, just in case the situation changes again and it cannot come about.

I remember listening to a lecture in Sydney given by Kathryn Greiner, wife of the then NSW Premier, and an influential city figure herself. It was at a school Speech Night and she was extolling the value of setting goals in one's life, taking hold of the tiller and not just letting oneself drift, shifted by every current and wind. I was going through a painful, disorienting divorce at the time and very much in a state of transition. And although only in my early 30s, in my bleakest moments I felt I was already too old to have any kind of attractive or exciting goals any more. My first reaction was to be very defensive, almost resentful towards her message.

But as I listened, I began to think of the range of things I still did have to look forward to. Some activities and opportunities that, in fact, I could not have aspired to earlier, nor in my previous situation. I don't think Kathryn's message was actually so much about the strict planning side of goal-setting, but about the value of Hope and the energy of Desire. It was about thinking big, having dreams and most especially having the courage to give yourself permission to set them as intentions.

Unfortunately it can be very easy to confuse setting intentions with planning which, during times of transition and uncertainty, can seem too rigid and irrelevant to a fluctuating situation. So by letting ourselves avoid what looks like planning and a likely irrelevancy, we may miss out on embracing intentions which can ultimately offer us a short-cut out of the unsettling transition – and straight into Significance.

The Oxford University Press *Philosophical Dictionary* defines 'intention' as being in a state of mind that is favourably directed towards bringing about some state of affairs, but which is not a mere desire or wish, since it also sets the subject on a course to bring that state of affairs about. The beauty of that as an approach, as teachers and philosophers from Dante to Dyer have noted, is that the journey is just as important as the destination.

I remember an occasion one year when I was on the Judging Panel for the *Sydney Morning Herald*'s annual True Leaders selection. We were being asked to choose the country's Top Ten business and community leaders. Various names were being discussed, and one particular panellist kept shooting down candidates with comments like, 'But he wasn't successful in quite a few areas' and, 'I wouldn't have said everything there had successful outcomes'. Eventually I felt I had to pose the question, 'But do all True Leaders have to *always* be successful? What about the importance of their intentions, and the influence their quest can have on others?'

His instinctive response was, 'Of course they have to be successful!' However, it moved us into a valuable reflection on whether that meant many of our most revered role models would never have been allowed on to our list: Jesus would have been hard pressed to make it to the shortlist for several hundreds of years, Mother Teresa could have been a non-starter for not curing poverty or touching everyone's life in India, and Winston Churchill would have had a career which was far too chequered for that panellist's taste.

Intention is the substance of Significance. It is about the outcome *and* the process. In fact the process, or journey, has a special power of its own. Following your intention, you become a role model by the way you do what you do. If the intention is concentrated strongly enough on the desire it becomes, in that lovely phrase, 'So important that it's worth risking failure for'. In contrast, when a goal or an aim is all about outcome, the danger is that it can lead to 'the end justifies the means' philosophy.

***

DEVELOPING THE GAMEPLAN:
Seek your own significance

Questions & activities to help you define the
influences on you to date, how you have made
decisions about life and career, and open up
possibilities for a bolder significance in
the Second Half

---

1. Making sense of earlier influences

To be fully conscious of how and why we are who we are at this point,
and to see clearly whether we are following our own path, or still caught
up in someone else's, it helps to reflect upon how we came to make the
decisions that we did.

How did you make your decision about your first job?
With hindsight, what influences were working on you as you made that
   decision and others in your early career?

What other options did you consider?
Why did you eventually make the decision/s you did in those days?
How do you feel about that?

What were other key events/periods of influence for you, after your first
   job?
After your first big promotion?
After your first child was born?
When you hit 40?

Do you feel you made a gameplan?
How did you go about it?

Or do you wish you had, but did not actually do so?
Is it something you consider going forward? If not, what are your
    preferences?

What would you have liked to have done differently in your life, if
    anything?

What do you see as patterns in how you have approached your life and
    career decisions to date?

Are there any lessons you can see which could be applicable to how you
    approach your next stage?

2. What do I really want to do? – Getting back to basics

Sometimes on the road to success we are tempted to concentrate so hard
on the tasks and the must-do's that we lose sight of what we actually *enjoy*
doing, or at least our repertoire shrinks considerably. I have very often
found that those who say, 'I work hard and play hard' actually have a very
limited number of 'play' activities: travel, good food, some holiday-related
sports. What they may well mean is, 'I play *expensively* to try to compensate
for the lack of time, thought and effort I give myself to devote to it'.

David Grayson is a social entrepreneur who moved into academia to
become a Professor at the age of 52 and is currently Director of The
Doughty Centre for Corporate Responsibility at Cranfield University. He
came up with an excellent thought provoker, which I find gets people back
to the basics of what stirs, interests and delights them. He calls it 50-4-50,
as it seems to have a special magic for a Big-O birthday. (Although I find it
works just as well for any age birthday you care to mention.)

He explained to me how the idea came about:

'Don't just celebrate your 50th,' said a good friend of mine, as we watched
the sunrise over Macchu Pichu, 'but do fifty things that you really want to

do.' So was born the idea to extend my celebration of my half-century! Other friends are already repeating the idea with several planning '40-4-40' and one has the goal next year of '60-4-60.'

It is, of course, entirely arbitrary, and you alone determine what should be on the list. Most I planned in advance, but some activities have been added in retrospect after I did them – and the 'year' stretched to cover from my 49th birthday to the eve of my 51st in May 2006.

Some of David's special things included getting to know Madrid, setting up a Talented Young Britain bursary for Britons with disabilities, having a full medical 'MOT', sitting for a photo shoot, trying water-skiing for the disabled, redoing the garden and seeing five foreign films. (For more information see www.davidgrayson.net)

With my own Big-O birthday coming up I have started making my own lists and doing some of the things on it. The biggest surprise, and disappointment in a way, was how hard it felt to get beyond 20 items. I'm sure it's not because I am already totally fulfilled and want nothing more from life. Quite the opposite. The difficulty is in remembering some of the things I *used to* enjoy before life got this hectic, and allowing myself to admit to some curiosities about trying something new, which I would normally think far too foolish to mention (such as learning the Maori Haka).

Giving oneself permission to look inside and reconnect with our own simple joys, passions and interests at this almost whimsical level is a great way to start opening up the heart and mind to the question: 'What do I really want to do?' Try it for yourself.

Whatever your next birthday happens to be, choose that number as your target (let's say 60) and think of 60 activities you'd like to undertake between now, that birthday and the following one.

Here are some suggestions to start you off:

Learning a new skill
A new place

Something you haven't done for years
An activity which needs courage or risk-taking
Something nice for someone else
Trying out a sport
Something which pushes you out of your comfort zone
What others might interpret as 'out of character'

What does your list look like?
Who do you want to share some of the adventures and activities with, if anyone?

Think back to when you were somewhere between 12 and 15 years old.
What did you think you wanted to be when you grew up?
How does that sit with what you did over the next 40-odd years?
Are there any dreams or ambitions you 'gave away' or lost during your teens that you would like to revisit or regain?

If you could sit down with the young adolescent that you were then, what advice would you give him or her?

Imagine you are 95, and could sit down with yourself as you are today. What advice would you give yourself? What would help or hinder you in taking up that advice?

3. From success to significance

I believe that everyone can discover their Significance. That is, *discover* or uncover it. The answer is inside all of us already.

Some people worry that they will look selfish or arrogant if they attempt to articulate it, others are sometimes concerned that they will not be able to live up to what they wish to pursue. Those fears make it very hard to do the *discovering*.

But in the words often attributed to Nelson Mandela:

> Our deepest fear is not that we are inadequate. Our deepest fear is that we are powerful beyond measure. It is our light, not our darkness that most frightens us. We ask ourselves, 'Who am I to be brilliant, gorgeous, talented, fabulous?' Actually, who are you not to be? You are a child of God. Your playing small does not serve the world.

Here are some questions which are worth pondering, and which will help you start to discover and articulate what Significance can mean to you, as you move beyond Success.

Some will resonate with you more than others. Take your time over these, as this type of reflection is most fruitful when left to germinate and reviewed iteratively.

Fill in the gap/s:
   If I could . . . . my life would have meaning.

Change 'What can I do?' into *'What needs to be done?'* Then ask yourself the question.

Imagine it is the tenth anniversary of your death. A biographer has been given full access to your friends and family, important documents and photographs, letters, newspaper clippings and information about your work, your volunteer activities and political and community involvements.

Now imagine that *you* are that biographer and have sifted through all the material.
What would you say about the subject?
What kind of person was he/she?
What were this person's values and goals?
What did he/she believe in and stand up for?
What did the subject offer to the world (family, community, etc.), and what did they ask in return?

Next, ask yourself how happy you would be with your biography? What
do you still have time to change to ensure it presents the person you
want to be at the end?
How can you start that process right now?

On what occasions have you felt most fulfilled and 'on purpose' in your
life to date?
What pattern/s can you see in those circumstances?
How can that understanding inform your pathway to Significance?

What words have you lived by, and which act as your calibrating
mottos?
Someone's advice, good or bad?
Song lyrics or lines of poetry which have guided your actions?
What do they mean to you? What moved you to choose them?
Is there any phrase or motto which comes to mind particularly regarding
your future?

4. For further practical assistance on discovering 'What next?'

Whether you are already excited by the opportunities that are opening up
in your mind about the Second Half, or still needing more time and support
to *discover* and articulate what they may be, here are some further
recommendations.

For those who feel they work best alone, at their own pace and through
visual images, I think there is no better structure than Mind-Mapping,
invented by Tony Buzan. His frameworks are exceptionally useful for
expanding and clarifying options, and at the same time getting to the heart
of an issue. I highly recommend his books. See which publications appeal
to you most and gather more information from his website:

www.buzanworld.com

If you prefer the idea of a more experiential and facilitated process to help
you flesh out exactly what your preferences and possibilities could be, here

are two organisations which offer short programmes to assist. They will be very familiar with the concepts of Generativity and Significance, and the issues around later-career. The courses can be done as individuals, couples or in small groups.

I have worked with both and find their processes can create some genuine breakthroughs in recontacting with a sense of purpose and meaning:

www.senssoma.com

The creators of Senssoma describe it as being about accessing one's desires and intentions from a whole new perspective. For me, its power is that it cuts through the more usual and logic-focused 'leadership' and self-development programmes. It is a process which allows participants to step outside the box of normal every day awareness and draws from the wisdom of the body and sensory awareness to allow them access to their true values and drivers.

Through it many discover that what they think 'logically' are their goals, are not really aligned with who they are. In Senssoma, the point is to explore the 'who' so that a whole new perspective opens up. Priorities are clarified, barriers lifted and decisive action is freed up. People find themselves more creative and engaged in their lives, and able to integrate work and life in an authentic and satisfying way.

It is a process which can be used by corporates and individuals alike.

www.passionmaps.com

Peter Wallman, founder of Passionmaps, describes the importance of some sort of intervention to assist in making the most of the Second Half.

> Many feel released from the questions with which we may have been pre-occupied for years if not decades, ie 'How do I best make a living and pay the mortgage?' or 'How do we best raise our children?'.
>
> The questions that can now come into sharp focus can be 'What should I do to gain the most fulfilment with the rest of my life?', and 'What can I do that makes life most meaningful for me and give me the sense that my life counts?'.

As a qualified Passion Map facilitator myself what I like about the Passion Mapping programs is that they address these new questions by first getting to the essence of each of our unique passions, and discovering the pattern which connects them all. By connecting deeply with the energy of their passions, individuals (and couples) are able to create a clear and holistic vision which brings all their passions alive. They are also guided into articulating what makes their lives most meaningful and gives them the certainty that their life really counts. So, both individually (or as a couple) they can acquire the tools to proactively design and live their lives from the uniqueness of who they are, what is most important for them, what they want to achieve and who they want to become.

Through the process many individuals find a new zest for life. Many couples, in particular, find that by reconnecting with their shared passions through the programs, they have been able to spark a new relationship based on what they love to do together. Sometimes programs bring up surprising new possibilities, sometimes the programs bring a sense of confirmation of being on the right track and learning about letting go of unnecessary activities.

Passionmaps works with individuals, couples and organisations, counting McKinsey as one of their global clients. According to Peter Wallman, 'The highest assessment scores come from the relationship programs which usually are ranked 5 out of 5. So I think renewing relationships in mid life is a huge and often unspoken issue.'

Suggestions for those who either feel they know what they want to do and/or would like a support network for the process include the following programmes:

www.sbs.ox.ac.uk/execed/leadership/what-next/Overview.htm

'What Next?' is an intensive five day programme run by Said Business School in Oxford and Common Purpose, the Social Leadership organisation, in the UK. It is aimed at those experienced in leadership positions who are within a few years of leaving, or have recently left, their senior roles and are wondering what they will do next. For anyone preferring to put their energy and leadership experience to work in society, rather than just retire from professional life, this programme offers both inspiration and practical first steps.

Participants describe it as a chance to rethink individual values, explore the risks and challenges of non-executive roles through the insight of the experienced advisors, all in the company of a peer group who share a passion to somehow make the world a better place.

My own organisation also runs occasional Public Programmes for individuals in later-career, and tailor similar programmes for corporate in-house useage. We also consult to organisations in the private and public sectors on all aspects of Extended Careers including data collection and analysis, policy development, implementation, individual and group coaching and later-career leadership development. For more details go to:

www.CGAcademy.org

6

Your legacy to the game
OR
Leverage your platform

One of the most enjoyable parts of being a high performer, as we have said throughout the book, is the success it brings with it. That may take the form of money, power, achievement, recognition, lifestyle, fulfilment or a mixture of all of them. So one of the hardest things for high performers to contemplate is what on earth could be as exhilarating as success. What could possibly replace it? The answer, across the board from Jim Collins to Deepak Chopra, is moving from Success *for self* to Success *for a greater community*. Or, acknowledging the influence of Generativity, it could be phrased as the chance to move from Success to Significance.

I have occasionally found some people to be dismissive of the idea of Significance, mistakenly associating it only with voluntary work, or a lower level of intellectual or creative engagement or as some form of soft-edged philanthropy. In the course of writing this book it in fact seems to have been the self-proclaimed 'hard-nosers' who feel most affronted by the idea that Significance could be as, or more, attractive or awesome than the Success they have achieved in their First Half.

Yet the clincher and view-shifter is to ask those 'hard-nosers' whom they most admire. Who are their all-time role models, of any age? The Top Ten usually includes people like Nelson Mandela, Mother Teresa, Albert Schweizter, Mozart, Kennedy, Churchill, Martin Luther King, Lech Walesa and Rosa Parks.

Strangely, businesspeople rarely feature on the lists. Bill Gates and Henry Ford are two of the few exceptions. And their names never come up because of the money they amassed, but for their significance. They mention how

Gates has channelled his wealth into global educational and socio-economic projects and how Ford revolutionised our 20th century lifestyles by making cars an affordable commodity.

Values and meaning

I have only occasionally heard anyone bring up Donald Trump or Samuel Walton as a person they greatly admire, and then only rather sheepishly in jest. Again, the clincher is the question: 'Would you rather your children remembered you as being like Trump or like Mandela?' It's a no-brainer. The question touches the part of us where meaning matters, and our heart as well as our logic is involved.

From the values and meaning point of view, Significance trumps mere Success every time. It is surely the perfect quest for those who have achieved Success to their heart's content already. And for those who feel that true Success has eluded them in the First Half, it offers a compelling new target to switch to.

Besides, as I have pointed out throughout the previous chapters, developmental psychologists and philosophers agree that to progress to the next level of development one does not have to stop being who and what one was before. Every phase transcends and incorporates what has been built before. Moving to Significance, by any criteria, is about becoming intellectually, emotionally and spiritually larger not smaller.

Let us go back and look at Significance as achieving something meaningful for the greater community. The greater community can be your team at work, your family, your field of expertise, the community in which you live. It does not necessarily have to be what may be called a philanthropic cause at all. Although, by the same token, there should equally be no reason why Significance should *not* be a target in the form of a philanthropic BHAG, a Big Hairy Audacious Goal, like a cure for cancer, improving conditions for indigenous peoples or increasing educational opportunities for the disadvantaged.

So what do I mean by a platform and how can it best be leveraged for Significance?

Our platform is the power base from which we work to make something happen. I have regularly heard it used in the contexts of business and political leadership, I feel I learnt the real meaning of the term when I was on the Sydney Leadership Programme run by the Benevolent Society in NSW, Australia in 2003. As I understood it there, it is the combination of one's profession and position, one's personal, professional and interest-based networks, the resources and assets one has at one's disposal, and a variety of other 'tools' such as one's reputation, persuasiveness, credibility, etc.

On that programme I met a number of unforgettable role models who used their resources to genuinely *move towards* making a difference, and I had the privilege of working alongside many of them on the course. Among them were Danette Fenton-Menzies and her husband Graeme, who contributed financially and in kind to a variety of causes. They were certainly not wealthy in the business tycoon sense of the word at all, but could invariably be relied upon to assist with monetary sponsorship for 'unsexy' causes like drug rehabilitation projects in South Sydney, and offering their farm for R&R and training events for other organisations. There was also Mark Yettica-Paulson, one of the new band of aboriginal leaders in Australia who remains one of the greatest encouragers, teachers and ambassadors I have ever met, and one of the most generous with his time and wisdom. His humility and grace are simply inspiring.

The importance of *moving towards* your aim

And I use the words *moving towards* making a difference on purpose, because one of the greatest temptations we can succumb to is believing that anything less than total, achieved success must somehow be failure. It is related to the passion-dampening excuse that big problems cannot be fixed and that one person cannot make a difference to them . . . so why start?

To me it seems counter-intuitive to hear senior business people and public sector officials voice that self-limiting belief, and so avoid engagement on some of the really meaty 'big issues' which affect our lives – like education, poverty, health, justice, corruption, prejudice, etc. I look at their backgrounds and achievements and see many times when they have carried on with initiatives in the work arena, and seen them through, against the toughest odds. And also when they've spent nights on end building business cases or crafting tenders, only to find them rejected – yet not flinching because 'if a goal is worth fighting for, it's a goal worth failing for'.

One person whom I asked about this paradox countered with, 'Yes, but we did that for the money!' She then reflected and added, 'Well, actually, no. If it's just a monetary incentive it somehow doesn't evoke the same energy. This was a great telecoms innovation and we did it because we really believed we had a great product and could fundamentally change the way people did business if they bought it. The first potential client took a cheaper option, but we gave it our best shot and that's what mattered. And we believed in it so much, we just kept on and on until gradually we started to sign up users. Then the momentum carried us.'

The field of sports is full of this philosophy in action. Where else could the phrase, 'Give it your best shot' come from? It should never be forgotten that someone who has an intention, and sticks to it, successful or not, can be just as memorable in creating a worthwhile role model as a world or Olympic champion.

Gavin Freeman, a long time senior psychologist on the Australian Sports Commission and author of *The Business Olympian* (Freeman, 2008), characterises the attitude of the most successful athletes:

> They often say 'Many of the athletes whom I competed against in school had natural talents that were far superior to mine, but they gave up. The difference is that I didn't.'

Take Milt Campbell, the black American athlete. Against the odds at the Olympics of 1952, in Helsinki, Finland he won a silver medal in the decathlon, one of the most stamina-testing of events imaginable. But a silver medal was still one place short of where he wanted to be. At the next Olympics, Milt came to Melbourne, Australia. For four years he had been the reigning silver medallist, second best in the world, but committed to being the very best. In all the intervening time he concentrated on reaching his goal. He finally achieved that, winning the gold medal.

Roger Bannister, the British runner, was selected as an Olympic 'possible' in 1948, but preferred to set his sights on the 1500 metres for the same 1952 Helsinki Games. He had been impressive over the previous two years, and ten days before the Olympics had run a three-quarter mile in 2:52.9, but he was thrown by a late decision to have semi-finals. He qualified fifth from his heat and, although he set a new British record in the final, he missed the medals by one place. What history remembers him for, of course, was continuing doggedly and making up for it two years later with the first sub-four-minute mile, which he went on to lower to 3:58.8 in the 1954 Commonwealth Games.

There is a further, even more powerful message in sport. An occasion where the courage of a loser shines even more inspirationally for the heart and soul and commitment they put into their effort.

At the Australian Olympics in 2000 the home crowd was just as moved and inspired by its heroes who did *not* win gold as by Ian Thorpe and Cathy Freeman who did. The values and attitude that shone through were just as compelling as those of the winners themselves in impacting on others' aspirations.

Jai Taurima, who ultimately won the silver medal in pole-vaulting, was a delightfully colourful character who seemed, on the surface – with his long hair, navel ring and cigarettes – to be the antithesis of the clean-cut Olympian. Yet he always looked as if he was having the time of his life and ended up jumping an amazing 14 cm further than he had ever jumped before. He had originally been way out of the reckoning for a medal, and was an inspiration because his passion carried him further than he had ever dared to hope.

It was the same thing at the cycling, where Australia's Michelle Ferris raced her heart out over 500 metres, smashing a five-year-old personal best. She didn't win the gold medal, either, but for her and her supporters that didn't matter. She did more than she had ever done before, and surely that is all that anybody can ask. As she put it: 'I don't care what happens because I've killed my PB (personal best).'

She did everything she could to win and got beaten, and there is no shame in that. Some would say there is even more courage and greatness of heart in that than for the superstars who know they will go home with a medal, come what may.

What a sad state of affairs it would be if no-one ran a race in case they might get beaten, or left the field ashamed instead of elated when they had truly given their best but failed to beat a better opponent. It should be the greatest cause for pride – the true Olympic spirit.

Pushing the peanut forward

That brings me back to something else which gave me a new perspective on using our platforms. It was the invitation to allow oneself to *move towards* making a difference, even if it looks like a Herculean task. To start trying, even if it looks obvious that the ideal ultimate success can never be attained.

On the Sydney Leadership Programme we had some excellent background reading materials. A piece which particularly stirred me introduced me to the notion of 'pushing the peanut forward'. It was the title of a chapter in a book by Peter Singer, entitled *How Are We to Live?* (Singer, 1995).

In it, Singer tells the story of one of the great champions of Herculean tasks, Henry Spira, the Coordinator of Animal Rights International. An activist for more than 50 years, he fought for union democracy in the maritime industry, marched for civil rights and, in his 60s, he moved to animal rights campaigning and won major battles to reduce animal suffering. He was instrumental in persuading Revlon to stop testing cosmetics on animals and convinced major companies like Procter & Gamble to invest millions in research for alternatives to animal testing. In the years before he died, Spira felt like a lone voice protesting against transport and living conditions for food animals. He used the term 'pushing the peanut forward' about the uphill struggle he found the animal rights issue to be.

He was always fully aware that his fight was not popular, and that anything he was likely to undertake could only ever be a partial success. But was that worth throwing in the towel for him?

> The reality is that nine billion non human animals are being raised on farms every year for dinner. For as long as they remain edibles it is both futile and counterproductive to engage in the blustering bravado of 'Abolition now!' Progress is made stepwise, incrementally. Pushing the peanut forward. You can have ideals, but, in practical terms, what are you going to do today? What are you going to do tomorrow? It's crucial to have a long-term perspective. Looking back over the past 20 years, I see the progress that we've helped achieve. And when a particular initiative causes much frustration, I keep looking at the big picture while pushing obstacles out of the way: *pushing the peanut forward.* And there's nothing more energizing than making a difference.

As I mentioned earlier in the chapter though, the focus for significance does not need to be a major social issue. It can be a legacy you leave for the business you are in. For John McFarlane, CEO of ANZ Bank in Australia, it was a mission to leave the retail banking world a better place, operationally and ethically. As the head of one of the country's most influential financial institutions he used his platform extraordinarily effectively to hasten that.

In our interview he clearly resonated with the qualities inherent in Generativity, and made no bones about aspiring to them:

More and more I ask myself: why am I here? I am here for a purpose. Everyone is. I know I have not yet fulfilled it. I've a lot of years ahead and I believe it is my responsibility, but also my privilege, to be a contributing member of society beyond banking too. I intend to use today as a foundation, just as I used yesterday as my foundation to get to where I am now.

He recognised what a gift Generativity can be too, when harnessed for an organisation's good. Part of his legacy to the bank was a series of bold initiatives to offer longer, more fulfilling careers to his bank staff as part of an overall diversity policy. And another part was a legacy to the broader community, through being a member of the Prime Minister's Task Force on workforce ageing, and extending his mission of diversity beyond the ANZ organisation.

The point is finding meaning. It's the meaning which sparks energy.

Another ex-candidate of mine took meaning and a sense of achievement from a much smaller vision, closer to home. 'It may seem like it was peanut-sized, but it seemed worthwhile to me!' he said.

Looking back, the only regret I think I had about my career was that I didn't spend enough time with my kids. I always seemed to end up finishing a report instead of going to swimming practice, or finding I'd got a breakfast meeting with a client on the first day of term and not taking my daughter to school. The worst moment was arriving far too late at a Christmas Concert where she was performing a solo, because I 'had to' stay back for an internal meeting.

I didn't want to let down my boss I suppose, although had the other engagement been a client neither of us would have thought twice. But however angry I might have imagined my boss could have been about my leaving early it couldn't have been as bad as the look on my little girl's face because she knew I'd missed her big moment. It was just some big awful bind I'd got myself into and I didn't know how to get out of it.

So when I started thinking about the type of legacy I wanted to leave for the firm, and what I could influence to change, I thought I'd like to help stop others from getting themselves in that bind. My daughter had had her own child by that time, so I decided to be there for him at the start of every term. I'd offer to collect him when my daughter might have to work late. And I took time to go to every doctor's appointment with my wife when she had a cancer scare recently – which, she reminded me, I certainly hadn't done in similar circumstances a few years ago.

And you know what? I can truly say it *did* make a difference. I had women come up to me and say that because I set a precedent, as one of the most

senior *men*, it set a tone that made it acceptable for them to do it too. I had
men come up as well, and thank me, and say they had always wanted to before,
but felt it would be unacceptable to arrange matters so they could go to family
events. And I never had anyone take advantage.

It felt like it was the least I could do. I knew that with my position, my
authority and no worries about whether it might possibly damage my promotion prospects I could show my priorities with impunity. There were a few
who probably thought it meant the old fella was slowing down, but in my
mind that's just an excuse for avoiding the main point: Healthy priorities!

I had the platform to be able to do that. If I didn't, who else could or
would?

All the same, it can be only too easy to side-step an opportunity to create
precedents which go against the prevailing culture.

Jeremy, a Functional Head in a large UK business reflected to me, several
years after he moved from the company, that he wishes he had been more
vocal in countering popular prejudices:

I'd been as politically incorrect as anyone, I suppose, about the old fogeys
moving aside earlier for us young turks to come through. I never gave a
thought to where they might move aside to, or how they'd feel about that
themselves. When they went it was out of sight, out of mind. I joined in
carping about how so-and-so was losing his energy, and how we couldn't carry
anyone who wasn't as productive any more. Then of course there came a time
when it gradually dawned on me that I was turning into one of those old
fogeys myself.

I don't know why I just carried along with the game. Looking back, I
suppose I thought that if I continued to join in with the banter, I might
somehow look as if I wasn't 'old' myself. Everyone else my age could be old,
just not me. I suppose I didn't want to call attention to myself. I wonder,
though, if I didn't just end up looking rather foolish.

One thing the experience certainly did for me was help me understand
what my wife had been going on about all these years, about how uncomfortable she felt in the middle of genderist banter, and how difficult it was to
know how best to react. I used to think she was being too sensitive, and that
it was all good-natured ribbing. But having been on the receiving end of 'old
bloke' ribbing, I know there's an edge to it which goes beyond a joke, and
isn't funny at all when you know you are perceived as fair game, and find
yourself in the minority.

What legacy to leave?

I am often asked to talk about the subject of leaving a legacy. Not of the
monetary sort, but involving oneself in meaningful, generative activities

which can be either incorporated into one's current work or extended beyond it. It does not surprise me at all when members of the audience look at me ruefully and admit that they simply have no idea what that might look like for them. Having often been workaholics, focused totally on the job in hand, they have been blinkered to the options around them. In many cases they have been out of practice in connecting with their personal passions and interests for so many years, that they have simply forgotten what they were in the first place.

It was the same in Executive Search, as David Nosal agrees:

> I used to think that when people in later-career asked me 'What can I do now?', they wanted to use me as a sounding board. I came to understand however, over the years, that they genuinely were asking because they didn't feel they knew. That's really sad. It means they didn't really get to know themselves, and they didn't take the time to cultivate an outside life.

In my research a very common concern which comes through in later-career is how light-on many feel about having any genuine, worthwhile passions to pursue, whether now or in the future. Worries surface about 'Having no direction any more', 'Only being involved in inconsequential stuff' or 'Not knowing where to start or what I could find to excite me, if not the job I'm doing'.

I start with one very simple suggestion. Look at what your firm is doing about Corporate Responsibility and Sustainability, not just for the business itself but how that then links with broader economic and ecological Sustainability policies and activities. Find out what its policies are on engaging with the broader community. You will find that these days most companies are moving well beyond the tokenism of raising money for charity, and are working closely with a wide range of external stakeholders on a variety of social, economic and political issues designed for mutual benefit.

A good starting point would be to look at the Business in the Community (BITC) and Doughty Centre websites for more information: www.bitc.org.uk and www.doughtycentre.info.

It constantly surprises me that some of the last people to cotton on to the genuine challenge and stirring opportunities inherent in Sustainability are those in their Second Half. It fits perfectly as a vehicle for the journey towards Significance, and requires an approach which both incorporates and transcends the basic attributes for business success. One explanation seems to be that for much of their First Half, they would have been formed within cultures which looked at anything except the pursuit of shareholder monetary gain as a distraction to the business. As ever, achieving something worthwhile often means having to rewrite one's internal, often previously unconscious, script.

The outcomes of active involvement have clear three-fold advantages: to a business, to the world at large and to the individual for finding meaning and engagement in something which stirs his or her desire to create a just and values-aligned future.

Leveraging the platform

Of course involvement can come in paid, partly-paid or voluntary form. It can come whilst still in one's long-term career or beyond it. But when I was in head-hunting there was one piece of advice we always used to give: try never to resign without having a job to go to. In other words, start the hard work while you still have your platform, or power base, intact and at its strongest.

The power of claiming one's platform whilst in a leadership role, whilst retaining full authority to effect change, will also have the added benefit of helping one eventually move more smoothly and purposefully into one's own next steps.

One high-profile example is that of Ray Anderson, at Interface. When he set up Interface Inc. in the USA in the early 1970s he admits that he wasn't concerned about the environment. 'I just wanted to survive in business,' he says in his book, *Mid-course Correction: Toward a Sustainable Enterprise: The Interface Model* (Anderson, 1999). Around the start of his own Second Half, it appears he read Paul Hawken's *The Ecology of Commerce*, in which the central argument is that industry is destroying the environment, and the only way to turn that around is for the industrial leaders to take a stand and change their approach to conduct their operations more responsibly.

Ray's carpet and floor-covering business was a billion dollar business, producing immense amounts of waste water and nearly 900 pollutants. It was not at all unusual in that industry, but with his new mindset he embarked upon reducing this mega-scale waste and conserving energy through recycling and solar and wind power. By investigating ways to reduce damaging waste and depleting resources, the company came up with partnerships with other companies to produce carpet tiles made out of corn waste. Such double savings, and the proof that businesses can protect the planet's resources whilst increasing, not decreasing profits, are at the heart of the philosophy he developed and expounded in his book.

Like Dick in Chapter 5, he moved from seeing his involvement as something one did in one's spare time to being interwoven with the good of the company, and the broader community too. Both moved from feeling that one insignificant individual could not make a difference to seemingly entrenched systemic problems, to seeing the significance and power in innovatively linking 'good' with 'business'. Generativity in action. As Ray Anderson said to an audience in Houston, 'It's not just the right thing to do, it's the smart thing to do.'

In earlier chapters I have quoted Dr Pat McCarthy and his research on later-career. His own story, too, is a great example of leveraging one's platform at that point in the career:

> When I was 52, the organisation that I had worked with for about 30 years began new succession planning initiatives to protect it from the expected exodus of baby boomers as they began to retire. Although I had no retirement intentions, I felt that I was being excluded because of my age and what I felt was flawed management thinking. The organisation would not enter meaningful discussion.
>
> I was enjoying the benefits of a successful career with significant achievements, salary increases were guaranteed, there was no risk to my employment, I was well placed organisationally, and I had taken steps to ensure that my skills remained current. Despite this, I felt that the end of my productive working life was close and there was little that I could do about it.
>
> Initially I was angry about my powerless situation. Gradually the anger passed but I became increasingly frustrated with an overwhelming feeling that I was wasting my life. I did not want to become merely an observer of life as it passed by me; I wanted to continue to be an active participant in it.
>
> In earlier times I had had a strong internal locus of control – I had generally felt that I was the master of my own destiny, rather than being reliant on the organisation to provide opportunities for me. I did not like the new feeling of being a puppet to the organisational puppeteer. I had long held a personal goal of growing into a statesman role as I aged. I had planned to achieve this through my demeanour and through skilful contributions to family and friends. Above all I did not want to be a black and white television in an era of 40 inch LCD colour televisions!
>
> Gradually I disengaged from my employer.

My earliest, and only, plan for easing into retirement involved a decision to identify a problem for me to work on over coming years. Problem solving was something that I wanted to do. As an additional benefit, I thought a substantial problem to think about would keep my mind active and perhaps would open other doors for me.

I had always been sensitive to the issue of older workers through my participation in a government/community initiative directed at better understanding the demographic changes impacting the developed world and its relationship to business. I was aware of anecdotal and academic evidence of widely held age based discrimination and stereotyping of older workers by society, and I knew that these underlying attitudes were dominant in many countries despite looming workforce shortages and consequential impacts on the country's GDP.

So when I was 54 I commenced a PhD focused on understanding why organisations seemed to waste their older human capital. The objective of my research was to understand older worker experiences of employment, and to examine the impact of those experiences on their motivation and effectiveness in today's organisations. My study compared the characteristics that global companies now look for in their workers, against the careers and personal aspirations of older workers. I also considered factors in older worker careers including reaching a career plateau, and the features of good job design and supervision.

At 57 I left the security of my long time employer to complete my PhD and to work in a less secure, part time position as an adjunct professor at a university. At age 60 I completed my PhD. Now, three years later I teach business leaders from China, lead a business mentoring program for young Master of Business Administration students, undertake a range of projects that include working on a team that is planning the refurbishment of a heritage building which is embracing innovation in classroom design, environmental sustainability and creative architecture. I am soon to commence supervising the research work of doctoral students. I participate in an international conference each year.

I'm happy that many doors continue to open for me and once again I am in control of my destiny, I am challenged by new learning and personal growth opportunities, and I am contributing to society. I am on track to be a statesman in my relationships with family and friends.

Perhaps best of all, I no longer feel any of the negative work related sentiments expressed by my peers, realities that characterised the last few years of my time at my previous, long term employer.

A special challenge

For high-performing business people and organisational chiefs, used to a 24/7 style of leadership, the step up from Success to Significance is also about harnessing the power of *interventionist* leadership. One can weave the attributes of Generativity seamlessly into the way one works every day. Yet the good news is that one does not have to be on duty all day to display, and bring benefit from, generative approaches. The opportunities can be just that: a series of interventions, targeted, defined and embraced.

Here I want to hold out a special challenge. For anyone feeling at a loss about what to leave as a meaningful legacy, I suggest you put your minds to improving the situation regarding Extended Careers. By doing that you have a ready-made opportunity to make an important impact on the lives of individuals, the performance of a business, its sector and the economy at large. Dr McCarthy's story revolved around how he is doing exactly that.

In any senior position one is in a position to analyse how the organisation views the subject of later-career, one has the authority to investigate the opportunities or barriers it puts up, and to hold up those examples to decision-makers, whatever age they may be, as open for improvement. The experience and, in the very best sense, the vested interest and understanding of the subject which one can bring when in the Second Half oneself, would give any related intervention special weight to succeed.

As in some of the examples here, you have the opportunity to use your platform to highlight issues, or you can opt to say they are so deeply systemic that you can do nothing. You can use your powers of persuasion, as well as your designated authority, to convince others that the myths they believe about people in later-career are unfounded. Even if you are not the CEO, as part of the management you are perceived to be an arbiter of culture and acceptable behaviour. What you support automatically has a seal of approval. What you don't question is likely to stand, and if you fail to raise the topic of later-careers on to the agenda it is likely to stay ignored or denied.

Let's first go to a sporting analogy to highlight the significance of championing a more appropriate attitude and set of practices around Extended Careers. You can probably think of a large number of elite athletes who have reached the very pinnacle of their sport – and how they have dealt with the change into becoming an ex-Olympian or ex-Super League or Test player, whilst trying to move into the next stage of their lives.

Some move gracefully from team captaincies into coaching or managing in the same sport, like Terry Venables in international soccer. Others have moved into totally different spheres, such as Mike Hawker, the ex Australian Wallaby who moved from Rugby Union into becoming the CEO of Australian Insurance Group (IAG), one of Australia's leading financial institutions. He has, incidentally, also become one of that country's prime movers in the cause of business sustainability and responsible business. He was recently, as he has been often, quoted on the importance of workforce sustainability as well as the aspects of economic and environmental sustainability. For him, that was something in a very different sphere.

Some wind down gradually, like David Beckham. Moving from his home country of England to Madrid then, once his career as an England player and Captain was unlikely to rekindle, moving to LA Galaxy. It was a highly lucrative offer, but he would no doubt still have had to wrestle with the assumptions about moving to a US club, and put up with comments from colleagues and the general public about it being either a sell-out or an admission of decline. However, being a $250 million 5-year deal, and given his stated intention of spending more time being an Ambassador for the game and coaching and training youngsters in the sport, it looks like a good model for Success beyond Success. (Not to mention pleasing his wife enormously by Brand Beckham becoming part of the glitterati of LA and on the fringes of Hollywood.)

Others retire abruptly, like Barry John the Welsh rugby star, at 28, citing the hype and the tension of being in the spotlight. He decided to give it all away with no fanfare, right at the height of his fame.

A sad number of the most driven and successful elite, however, retire from the game and hit the wall, like Diego Maradona, the legendary Argentine soccer player, who slumped – becoming for several years a sad figure of derision and pity. He had been the best of the best, but slid into drinking and putting on so much weight that he became unrecognisable from the lean, fit creature who had run rings around so many opponents.

Mark Henderson, US gold-medallist Olympic swimmer, told me about his experiences of transition:

> One day everybody wants your autograph, the spotlight is always on what you are achieving . . . then suddenly you have to go out into a new world where no-one knows who you are, and the only option looks like it's fetching coffees for guys 10 years younger than you. We may have said we'd be relieved when the limelight was all over, but the reality was that it took more getting over than we'd ever have thought.

What was very telling was that he added the comment that it was a situation that no-one warned him or his high-performing team-mates about. Nowadays Mark is an executive working in the global capital markets, and Chair of the US Olympic Team Athletes' Advisory Council, and he remains passionate about creating support structures for top young athletes to help them prepare effectively for that transition. He sees the parallels extremely clearly between what he went through during his sports retirement after the 1996 Olympics, and the lessons he'll take from it into later-career in his professional life.

Assuming that most readers are around the Second Half point of their lives, or further on, it is probably fair to assume that these sports stars would have been young enough to be their children at that particular point of transition in their lives.

So it will be easy to empathise with those young people, and feel compassion for the situation they found themselves in, coming to the end of their life at the top of the ladder. You can feel for them: the shame and disappointment of knowing their record-breaking days are over. The pleasure but also the pain of seeing younger, possibly less naturally talented, team-mates being picked ahead of them. The grief of knowing that they will never hoist the trophy above their head, and their potential in the chosen sport is now 'what might have been'. Relief that paparazzi no longer dog their every move, but also the twinge of ego when restaurant Maitre D's no longer recognise them and luxury goods promoters have stopped calling them up to try to persuade them to endorse their products. The sudden, sinking feeling that time has caught up with them and from now on their world will become unfamiliar, unknown territory. They find themselves in a place they had been too full-on and busy to bother to consider while caught up in the spotlight.

Whenever I tell the stories of Mark Henderson or Diego Maradona and their challenges in moving on from the peak of their sporting career, my executive listeners show great understanding and empathy for the athlete's predicament. They comment compassionately on the psychological impact that retiring either at the peak, or winding down and winning less often, would have on these young people. They immediately identify the waste of talent and energy if these young heroes just dwindle away after scaling the heights.

They can see their sons or daughters in them, and have splendidly sensible advice for them. And they are often shocked and disturbed to hear there is little, if any, assistance in preparing or support for top sports stars in moving *beyond* their 'Glory Days'. In fact, I have found some of them even wondering how they, or their firm, could actively help improve the situation for these young champions. But, strangely, very few give themselves permission to see *themselves* in the same position as the Olympic stars. Yet they are.

It is true that even minor league, weekend players can suffer depression and anxiety as they start to notice that they are losing their edge, or that younger upstarts are taking their place on the side. But the stress and level of responsibility are vastly different for them than for those in the top ranking limelight. They are not defined by what they play, unlike their elite counterparts, nor so time-consumed by it; and their 'day jobs', however dull, give them an anchor and a safe place because they have always been carried on concurrently.

I wonder to myself, if these wise, compassionate executives want to take up cudgels to ensure that the world, and the individuals themselves, benefit from a sports 'elites' talents – why aren't those same people taking a stand on the benefits of the later-career 'elites'? Is the taboo around it still too strong to feel comfortable voicing those concerns? Is the sense of denial too deeply ingrained?

Luckily these days it is becoming more likely that the top sports men and women will receive preparation and coaching to assist them through the transition from top competitor and into a next step which will give them as much of the exhilaration, meaning and energy that their sports prowess gave them. Some national and international Institutes of Sport are beginning to offer such counselling. So do many clubs and even individual sponsors. I have also come across individual athletes who have sought and paid for such support themselves, not out of desperation or as a remedial option, but with the expectation of being super-charged through it and better able to gain their next version of Success.

Of course, it never used to be like that. The stars simply left and fended for themselves, for better or for worse. My theory is that the situation had nothing to do with the cost, and certainly nothing to do with spite or lack of concern. It was just that no-one had thought about it! The assumption was that as long as the guys had a bit of money behind them they would just glide seamlessly into the next phase.

Extended Careers – whose responsibility?

It's the same situation in business. Yet of the little light that *is* shone on performance, attitude and behaviour change in older workers, scarcely any is shone upon the executive and senior levels. Why is that, when the Beckham-like business stars are likely to suffer even more, and more publicly, from the pain of withdrawal, grief and under-occupation than their colleagues in what would approximate to the 5th or 15th side?

In the corporate world it is still generally assumed that if the leading executives have been paid well and have had a good title they will suddenly be able to metamorphose from a safe, solid, well-planned, well-managed upward career . . . into functioning in a totally unknown world, with no obvious structure or support. There is no logic in that, just naïve wishful thinking.

Very few organisations have caught up with the sport sector's good team management practices. Most no longer have a commitment to a 'duty of care' towards their staff, and the majority of companies still see any provision for training or job specification review to help enable Extended Careers as an unnecessary cost.

One company which is changing that outlook is BT. For a company that has, traditionally, encouraged early retirement in order to radically downsize the company, this is a huge shift in policy. The business recognises that mixed-age teams can deliver a better service to their customers. By bringing older and younger people together in a team BT believes it leads to much more diverse solutions, and their experience to date shows that they really enjoy working with each other. Their findings have been that it actually decreases the sense of 'Us' and 'Them' that they had been fearing – and the clients love it.

One of the options available to BT staff is flexible retirement, which enables people to gradually reduce their hours as they approach retirement and, as at December 2005, over 80% of BT employees showed an intention of working past the age of 60.

Their policy is now about valuing *all* their people's contribution, skill and expertise regardless of their age. As BT's People and Policy Manager Becky Mason commented:

> We could no longer sustain a retirement age, which meant skills and expertise were leaving for some arbitrary reason – and when they would have preferred not to go anyway. People do not suddenly become unable to do a job on a set retirement age. It doesn't make business sense not to retain loyal committed skilled employees if they want to stay on.

Other organisations retain a strong commitment to the welfare of their staff, which they incorporate into their policy and budgeting. In the UK the Metropolitan Police have a highly pro-active programme for their people, both officers and administrative staff.

Every month their HR support department runs a check to see how many staff will be eligible for retirement in exactly 12 months' time. The resulting report allows HR to contact all police officers aged 54, administrative staff aged 59 and all police officers a year away from 30 years of service with the Metropolitan Police Force, in order to make them aware of their options on remaining within the Force (The 30+ Scheme) and of the support and services available to them should they wish to retire or move on into an alternative career.

The support comes through a wide range of activities. There is a basic Information Pack which gives a comprehensive run-down on the options available to them, and recommendations for next steps and further contact. There are also a variety of Seminars, including retirement finances, self-awareness and self- and psychological assessment for career choice, ongoing internal opportunities, external job search assistance, self-employment opportunities. They have also created an Advice Centre and Library to which anyone in later-career can come for more personalised attention, plus a very high-touch one-to-one service for the most senior ranking officers, who very often use their police experience to move into other influential roles after 30 years with the Force.

What is particularly outstanding in their case is the take-up rate, given that all response from staff is purely voluntary. They estimate between 75% and 80% of all officers eligible for retirement take up some element or another of the advice offerings.

I consider this especially significant as it indicates a culture in which the 'age' and later-career taboo has been minimised, and that active involvement in later-career and Extended Career development has become 'normalised' (i.e. become 'the norm') within the organisation. It strongly indicates that when such a situation is created there is a real thirst for this kind of support. The pay-off is also that, through the new 30+ Scheme, the Police Service is extremely satisfied with its Extended Career retention rate.

Another aspect worthy of note is the Met's sensitivity to the needs of the different constituencies within the groups they target. In contrast, I have heard of a number of well-intentioned interventions which lose participants' trust and credibility – right from the start – by adopting a superficial one-size-fits-all approach. There are certain aspects which can be generic due to a shared stage in career, but differences in pay and superannuation/pension levels can make shared sessions extremely uncomfortable, even to the point of creating tensions where there were none recognised before.

In a similar vein, one recently retired C-suite executive I spoke to told me, extremely disdainfully, about his multinational company's attempts at helping him extend his vision on later-career/life opportunities:

> This nice little man kept going on about the hobbies we could develop. Ballroom dancing, for God's sake! Courses at the Library! If I'd realised I was going to be in this 'jollies' day with people who've reported to me for years, I would never have gone. It was embarrassing for all of us.

There may well have been an extreme element of snob factor in his reaction but, like any form of communication, it is imperative to gauge the audience and design an appropriate methodology. Missing the mark on that is ineffective at best, counterproductive at worst.

If you are considering a legacy in the form of ameliorating the situation concerning Extended Careers, there is a central riddle to solve. It is a point I have raised a number of times: whose responsibility is it to underwrite training costs or support research and innovative ideas for new approaches – employers, individuals or national economies (governments)?

Individuals obviously have a lot at stake, either needing to continue to earn money or to keep themselves happily engaged and active. Realistically though, it is a time in life, however well off a person may be, when many feel most risk-averse about spending money on their own development. And, as individuals, they do not necessarily know what would be the best approach to invest in for their own benefit.

From the philanthropic view, my ideal continues to be for employers to fund training and exploration of new ways to engage and use workers in extending career and productivity options. But so far my experience is that they seem highly reluctant to do so, regardless of how profitable they are. It's very much a 'what's in it for me?' reaction. And in that respect, I suppose they really do have a point. Of all stakeholders involved, they currently do not seem to have much vested interest and do not seem to feel any talent pinch yet.

National economies, however, and the likes of the EU, *do* have very strong vested interests – huge shortfalls in ability to pay pensions. It is in their interests to keep people working longer to avoid paying out so much, over so long. So, as the stakeholder with most to gain, one would have thought they might be best at 'investing' in better solutions.

In short, I contend that businesses, and their individuals, can come up with more innovative new options, and the government should take those best practices and actively incentivise roll-out of them via tax breaks and direct funding.

What governments, public and private sector organisations need is solid, well-informed, impassioned internal lobbying and advice on the subject. A cadre of persuasive senior, experienced leaders who can put forward the business case *including* the beneficial impact on overall Sustainability.

This is one perfect opportunity for later-career individuals willing to leverage their platforms and their experience to bring about change soon enough to be beneficial to their own Extended Career, but which will *definitely* benefit that of those to come. Could it be one cause you take up, a legacy you leave?

And what will be the others you choose?

***

DEVELOPING THE GAMEPLAN:
Leverage your platform

Questions & activities to help you work
out what your platform looks like, and how
it can be your springboard to significance
in later-career

1. What is your platform?

Very often we get into the habit of seeing ourselves as just 'someone
who does a job'. We can become blinkered to the special 'accessories'
and support structure we have to help us do that job, and the sophisticated
frameworks and networks we have built to run our lives over the
years.

Deconstructing all that shows us what our platform really is. It is usually
far more extensive, robust and valuable than people think before starting
the exercise.

It's like having Lego bricks. We spend time using the bricks to build, say,
a train station but then we get so used to what we've built that we only
see the station not the bricks that built it. But if we deconstruct that
station, we can see clearly again what bricks are at our disposal. Then we
can choose to build a garage, an apartment building, a cathedral or a
roundabout with those same bricks instead. . . . And as players at the top
of the game, should that cathedral need some more bricks for a spire,
you are more than likely to know what they need to look like and where
to get them.

So it is with understanding what your platform is, and possibly what else
may be of benefit to add.

What is at your special disposal if you wish to exercise your Generativity and/or create a legacy?

Career:
Authority?
Functional specialty?
Industry expertise?
Industry Association affiliations?
Educational qualifications?
Personal reputation?
Business travel opportunities?
Colleagues and connections?

External network:
External roles and authority?
Access to particular Clubs and Societies?
Access to influential/useful individuals?

Personal/organisational assets:
Property?
Vehicles?
Money?
Goods superfluous to needs?
General non-work-related skills?

2. 'Potlatch' – the significance of giving

Many indigenous tribes around the world share an attitude towards wealth which is very different from our own. Among the tribes of the Northwest coast of North America, the Chinook word 'Potlatch' (which I believe is how the word Potluck derives) means the auspicious time when a tribe chooses to assemble and give away to each other what they can afford to part with.

The generative nature, and beauty, of this event is that everyone gains a benefit. The receivers go home with the blankets, food or horses that they need and the givers gain the satisfaction of having given well and generously.

By later-career many of us are wealthy enough to give generously of our material possessions like that too, whether to our children, directly to the needier or to charities and other worthwhile causes.

By later-career, whether wealthy or not, we are in a unique position to borrow the spirit of the Potlatch and think on what we can give away in *non*-material terms too. This 'internal wealth' can be practical and tangible, like financial skills or project management or negotiation. And it can also be attitudinal and intangible, the sort of things that often lead people to be described as 'statesmanlike', like insight, compassion, good sense, prudence, warmth, humour.

> If you think of your Second Half as a Potlatch, what wealth will you bring to share?
> Money?
> Goods?
> Qualities?
> Skills?
> Experience?
>
> Exactly what will they be?
> Which ones do you feel most enthusiasm for giving away?
> Who needs them most?
> How innovative can you be about how you offer them?

3. Leaving a later-career legacy

The concepts of later-career and Extended Careers are still extremely new. There are very few templates to help us in how to tackle the subjects, and few role models.

The field is wide open to shape what those concepts should look like in practice. The very best experts are usually those closest to the themes.

Should you wish to use your platform towards these ends, and to leave a legacy, your choice is whether you approach it on individuals' terms, through your own organisation or sector, or through broader political and social agenda-setting. Or in combination.

Here are some thought starters.

Is the subject of later-career and, in particular, Extended Career, on the agenda in your organisation? If not, how can you use your platform to put it on there?
What sort of thought leadership would you like to see around it?

What is your own position on the theme?

How can you make a meaningful intervention, in your current leadership capacity, to benefit yourself and others – and also as a win–win for the organisation/society?

What do you see as some of the possible obstacles?
How can you 'sell' your case in terms of the benefits to all?
What else do you need to find out or investigate in order to pursue this?

7

Energy sources for a strong Second Half
OR
Sustainability: personal training for remaining a winner throughout

Throughout this book I have bemoaned the paucity of role models for us in our Second Halves. The truth of the matter is, however, that over the centuries there have been many inspiringly creative and influential individuals who have continued at the top of their game throughout their Second Halves, whom we would aspire to emulate. Yet because they were relatively few in number in any given period, that has made them seem as if they were exceptions.

Consequently, in our society we have come to believe that by later-career accomplishment and achievement fizzle out, and that they are the prerogative of youth. On closer inspection the math can disprove this theory completely. It was simply a case that *not many people at all lived into their 60s* and beyond until quite recently, so these inspiring creatives were in fact not exceptions, but *around the same ratio* as for any age group.

Sustainable careers

One of my favourite examples is that of William Marshal, a knight who lived in 12th century Europe (see Kaeuper, 2005). In the days when jousting and mêlées were considered professional 'sports' in the same way that we consider soccer or basketball today, William Marshal would have been Pele, Magic Johnson and Muhammad Ali all put together. He earned millions from tournaments and, later in life, as some of today's athletes do, like Lord Sebastian Coe, he was invited into politics eventually becoming Regent of England as protector to the nine-year-old Henry III.

What made him so special was not only the fact that he lived until his mid 70s, a good 20 or more years beyond the average at that time, but also that he led the victorious English forces against the French invaders at Lincoln only two years before he died. Accounts of the event tell that he was at the front of his men, charging at the French on his steed, killing one of the key French Generals and forcing the French King to surrender.

Great examples crop up across all fields. Somewhat different, somewhat less bloodthirsty, but no less active in terms of achievement are the examples of Agatha Christie, who continued to write until her death at 86 and Carl Jung, the pioneering psychologist. He continued to practise until his death, and completed his autobiography *Memories, Dreams and Reflections*, when he was 86 too. Mother Teresa of Calcutta won the Nobel Peace Prize aged 69, and continued active work and lobbying until 87.

Stradivarius, the renowned violin maker, is estimated to have made more than one thousand violins, cellos and violas between the age of 22 and his death at 93. Jacques Cousteau was writing and filming well into his 70s, and his final semi-autobiographical book *Man, the Octopus and the Orchid* was published just after his death at 87.

Other examples were pragmatists to the end. Etienne-Maurice Falconet was one of the most influential sculptors of the Rococo. When he had a stroke at the age of 67, he gave up sculpture but turned to researching and writing on art history, publishing nine volumes between then and his death at 71. Jeanette Rankin, as the first female member of the US Congress, served two terms, first in her late 30s, then in her early 60s. At the age of 87, in 1968, she led a group of 5000 women to march on Capitol Hill, Washington, DC to protest against the war in Vietnam.

The difference today is that there is a critical mass of people ready and able to undertake such feats for the duration of their Second Halves. People who are healthier and better educated than their age group has ever been before, and far more aware of the importance of motivation and purpose in playing even better in this half than in their first. The other day I was listening to a documentary on BBC Radio Four about the renowned Brazilian architect Oscar Niemeyer, sometimes referred to as 'The King of Curves' and the creator of the new mega metropolis of Brasilia (BBC News, 13 January 2008). He had turned 100 years old, and was still working actively and innovatively on new commissions.

On one level, because the critical mass is so new to our society, the challenge is that there are very few prior aspirational guidelines for this period of our lives. We have to make it up as we go, which means taking a risk and thereby it calls for some bravery.

The flipside of that is the freedom it offers, usually quite in contrast to the templates, rules and expectations, conscious and unconscious, of the First Half of our lives.

So the way you choose to express Generativity, and what you choose as your intentions for Significance, will shape you as a role model for others coming after you in their own Second Halves. I wonder what that overall, holistic picture looks like for you in terms of content? How will it all be bound together? And as all activities need to be fuelled by energy, where will your energy come from to put those intentions into action?

Fuelling sustainability

The importance of energy for fuelling the intentions from which one derives the sense of Significance is absolutely crucial. It is as important as the funding for them. That said, it is no more or less important than at any other time of one's life. We always need rich sources of energy, and to replenish our stores on a regular basis. Like cars we need to keep enough of the right fuel in our tanks or risk that feeling of running on empty, which is only too familiar whether we are stressed executives working 24/7, sleep-deprived parents of new babies or overwhelmed members of the caring professions such as teaching, nursing or peace-keeping. We've all heard it said, 'When it's all give, give, give . . . something's gotta give'. Even those who say they thrive on stress and have a high tolerance for hard and unremitting work admit that there comes a point beyond which one's performance deteriorates. A point where Success risks being compromised. Where relationships suffer and health becomes affected.

I would be extremely surprised if anyone reading this book has *not* experienced that sense of burn-out and running on empty at some point. Most often the excuses are, 'I didn't have time to recuperate' and 'I was too busy to do anything about replenishing my energy'. Those excuses can start at 15 and . . . often, sadly, end up in premature ill health or early death.

So my comments on needing to find and cultivate one's sources of energy do not reflect any concerns about diminished resources or sickness just

because of the ageing process. Rather, they are there to prompt better practices than you may have had to date. Nor is it meant in any way patronis-
ingly, about having more time on your hands now. The crux of the matter
is, 'Do you have the time now *not* to have the time?'

So what are the energy sources needed to keep you at the top of your
game throughout the Second Half? I've heard various versions of the things
we need to make a happy and fulfilling life. Some say: somewhere to live,
someone to love and something to do. Another version is that all we need
are health, money and love. They can be broken down into subsets, as in
the various NLP (neuro-linguistic programming) versions of the Wheel of
Life, which can include fun, learning and environment. Basically, they are
the ingredients which give us our energy.

The seven I use in workshops are:

• Finances
• Physical wellbeing
• Family and friends
• Fun and leisure
• Purposeful activity/work
• Continuous learning
• Self and spirituality

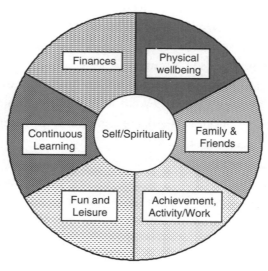

Figure 7.1 Energy sources

The point is that these are the fundamentals of the most effective training regime to maintain our overall fitness to perform, and the energy-providers which will enable us to keep at the top of our game throughout the Second Half.

Like any training regime, the closer you follow it, the greater the benefits to performance. If you continually postpone or cut corners, the impact is obvious. If any of you have ever blithely booked a skiing holiday, but never quite got round to the sit-ups and the hip and thigh-strengthening exercises, then you know exactly what I mean!

Once we get on to the exercises in the Developing the Gameplan section, you may find it useful to build your chart inclusive of subheadings, as it can be highly revealing. There was an 'Aha! moment' for Mark, a participant I remember who had scored himself as averagely satisfied with all the elements above. When he broke down physical wellbeing into: weight, fitness, diet and general health he realised he scored himself very low on weight and diet, yet high on the others. Then he looked at the scores he had given himself for lack of satisfaction with the hours worked, which were far lower than his sense of achievement.

The 'Aha! moment' for him was when he linked the two:

I always feel I don't have time to do anything about my diet, so my weight has been steadily going up for the last five years or more. And I snack when I am stressed, as I can tell myself I don't know when I'll be able to eat 'properly'.

The exercise forced him to take a decision to act on his weight issue, which was on the verge of causing him diabetes:

I've always blamed work, and said there was nothing I could do about it. But of course I have a choice. Several options in fact, now I know which levers I can pull.

It actually caused Mark to look at the work–time issue in more depth and explore exactly what the time–diet linkages were. It obviously wasn't merely a case of 'Work less, then!' but a call to identify when and how time pressure impacted on what he ate, and then find creative solutions.

Mark's example illustrates how the more conscious awareness we have of how we are faring in each of these categories, the greater our likelihood is to influence doing well in it.

Note that conscious awareness is subtly different from 'control'. There are likely to be some external forces on us in terms of time pressures, health, relationships, money, etc. which will be beyond our control. That always will be, and always has been, the case. We cannot control what happens to us. What matters is that we can control how we interpret what happens to us and, as a consequence, how we react to it.

Finances

Survival is the most basic of human needs and, in our society, money allows us that sense of security. There are numerous excellent books, websites and advisors which can help plan and implement effective Second Half financial strategies. It is not my specialty area at all.

My only advice, which I have repeated throughout the chapters, is for you to ensure that money and assets are kept in their place as *enablers* and *facilitators* for the bigger game, and not as an end in themselves. There is a discrete, but consequential, difference between asking, 'How much do I need to do X or Y?' and asking, 'To do X or Y, what do I need?' The emphasis on the latter focuses on the intention. What you genuinely need for it may have very little to do with money, and more to do with time, courage, persistence or commitment. Very often, the more successful we are as leaders and businesspeople, the more likely we are to only learn this if surprised by redundancy, bankruptcy or terminal illness or bereavement.

I was particularly affected by the recent autobiography *Chasing Daylight – how my forthcoming death transformed my life* (O'Kelly, 2007). It was written by the CEO of KPMG, a tremendously ambitious and successful achiever, in the short three-and-a-half months he lived after his diagnosis with a brain tumour, and was completed by his wife shortly after he died. In it he reflects on life, death, family, friends, himself and Nature, all as if through new eyes since his world changed so radically with the knowledge that he was about to lose the life he 'had been saving up for'.

One of the most moving insights concerned his spending – of time, not money. He had previously boasted of how well he managed his work–life balance, and that he always had time for his family and did lots of things with them spontaneously. He started to tell his wife how much he had enjoyed taking time out with her for lunches during the week. 'Do you realize how often you did that?' she asked him. He was mortified that, looking back through his diary, it turned out to be only about three times in over three years.

Worse still was when he looked at all the other names in the lunchtime slot over that same period, and couldn't recall who far too many of them were, nor why he had bothered to spend time with them. And most moving of all was his realisation that he had thought there were more occasions with his wife because he had remembered the feelings so vividly and how much he had enjoyed those lunches. They just hadn't made it into the priority list . . . back then.

Physical wellbeing

So, not surprisingly, along with money, physical wellbeing is one of the major concerns people of all ages seem to have about the Second Half. One of the obstacles we referred to in a previous chapter was the myth that older people/older workers get sick more often than their younger counterparts. In reality, until one reaches the mid or late 70s these days, the equation runs if you were healthy in your earlier years you will remain healthy. And if you were inclined to ill health, you are likely to remain that way too. Frankly, not that much changes.

Although one's eyesight may deteriorate and rheumatism or sciatica associated with ageing may increase, this does not tend to be as incapacitating as some of the unpleasant self-induced maladies associated with youth – like hangovers and sporting injuries.

In developed countries these days, the most 'dangerous' times to be alive are the first two years and the last two years of one's natural life. The rates for sickness and disease in the intervening years are largely random. The math goes that the longer you live, the longer you are likely to live.

It is always worthwhile to explode the myths about health in older workers and to take positive angles on health, but it is more important to view this as a pro-active training regime, meaning that the purpose is actually to *improve*. In the exercises at the end of this chapter you will rate your current health and fitness and devise an action plan to improve it. Not because it may be fashionable, but because it is fundamental to maintaining and improving one's capacity to be and do all one wishes in the Second Half.

Dieticians tell us that we tend to put on one to two pounds (half to one kilo) each year from our 40s onwards until we take conscious action to avoid it. It does not sound like much at the end of a year: 'Whew, I've only put on a couple of pounds or so this year'. But on a cumulative basis it can be mortifying: 'I'm nearly two stone/twenty-five pounds heavier than I was ten years ago'.

For some it takes a shock to the system, like an illness, bereavement or divorce, to lose excess weight. For others a new romance is the spur to renewed fitness and the increased energy and endorphins it brings with it. The most sensible can congratulate themselves that they have kept to a wise diet and exercise routine, and continue accordingly; and a few will decide, 'Enough's enough' and discipline themselves to knock off the pounds and make a fundamental readjustment to their lifestyle to keep it that way.

This is a way to create role modelling. A long-time friend of mine, when in his 30s was first pointed out to me as, 'The portly chap in the nice suit over there'. Now in his early 60s he has a better BMI (Body Mass Index) than back then, eats a far healthier diet and takes more exercise. Another old friend from Argentina of a similar age was scarcely recognisable, when I saw him in photos for the first time in over 20 years – for all the right reasons. He must have shed several stone, had no trace of his previously famed beer gut and overall looked as if he had not aged a single day since when we last saw each other.

George Vaillant, in his seminal work Aging Well, offers several recommendations for prolonging active, happy life. One of the most effective is simply to learn to feel happy in one's own skin. It helps to be physically, aerobically fit and lean rather than tubby but it can mean just as much to come to accept one's shapeless ankles and learn to feel proud of laughter lines. And, as we saw earlier, that advice is not merely anecdotal and wishful thinking, but distilled from the most exhaustive longitudinal study ever undertaken on causal factors not merely for longevity, but also for the quality of life involved.

The health and spirituality guru, Deepak Chopra, goes beyond this and asserts 'You can free yourself from aging by reinterpreting your body and by grasping the link between belief and biology' in his book Ageless Body, Timeless Mind (Chopra, 1993). His recipe is one of radical personal reinvention, in which he invites us to set aside all previous beliefs about the ageing process. As he so often says in his books and lectures, our bodies are constantly replacing themselves, cell by cell. The body that we each have does not have a single cell the same as it did four years ago, as they have all been replaced cyclically. If our cells are constantly regenerating, he says, they are regenerating to the same standard as they were before, if not better. It is only our minds and our assumptions (or self-limiting beliefs) which get in the way of continuing at peak health and performance.

Chopra claims that remaining healthy is actually a conscious choice. In his words, 'If you have happy thoughts, then you make happy molecules. On the other hand, if you have sad thoughts, and angry thoughts, and hostile thoughts, then you make those molecules which may depress the immune system and make you more susceptible to disease.'

The link between mental attitude, mood and health is well documented. By going on to link that to the ageing process, Chopra's views bear an uncanny resemblance to the findings from the rigorous research from Vaillant at Harvard, and the works of the founder of Positive Psychology, Martin Seligman. In addition to the physical sources of wellbeing of weight, fitness, diet and general health, they all propound the importance of the other less tangible, but equally valuable, sources of energy which contribute to overall wellbeing. These are our other headings of family and friends, achievements, activities and work, fun and leisure, self/spirituality and finances.

Family and friends

This is an area in which men and women seem to differ markedly, and where poor communication leading to unsubstantiated expectations and assumptions can cause intense disappointments. The greater consciousness one can bring to the subject therefore, the greater probability of happy outcomes – and a consistently satisfying, even increased, sensation of peak fulfilment.

Let's look first at the relationship with one's spouse or partner. It used to surprise me to find that so few men talked with their wives about their expectations for themselves and their relationships going into their later 50s, 60s and 70s, and instead rested on vague, unarticulated assumptions. Perhaps it should not have surprised me, as many of these men also confessed that they had never discussed the planning of their family with their wives either, regarding timing or number of children, or even contraception in between.

Back then, as much as in later-career, it seems such a waste of an opportunity, as men and women tend to come to the transition with different needs and viewpoints.

Gary was one such individual. He was extremely successful at what he did, a man of few words, basically a quiet introvert and with no-one outside his immediate family whom he would class as a friend. This did not worry him at all coming up to retirement. In fact he was looking forward to spending all his time with his wife of nearly 40 years. She, on the other hand, was waiting in trepidation for the day when he would be home for good. Unfortunately they had not thought (on his part) or perhaps not dared (on her part) to share their needs and expectations.

The strains soon began to show:

> It's just like having a kid around. He wants to come along wherever I go. I can't seem to get a moment to myself. He even wants to come along when I go out with my friend Marjorie, or when I just go round to her for a chat. He doesn't even *like* Marjorie, but he insists on coming. It spoils everything.

Gary was quite confused by the response he began sensing in Anne. He had taken it to heart when she had previously complained that he had been working too hard and too long away from home, and could not understand why she now seemed to resent his presence. He did not seem to appreciate that keeping her company was not an ON/OFF switch of all or nothing, and that they could work on fine-tuning the amount of time together that felt best for both of them. He interpreted Anne's desire for occasional time without him as a personal rejection.

As far as he was concerned, she provided all the friendship he felt he needed. While she was available to him, he felt no urge to look for any other friends or acquaintances. In contrast, for Anne, although she had been looking forward to *more* time with Gary, she began to feel claustrophobic because he seemed oblivious to her need for a certain amount of time and space to herself.

Neither of them had been used to voicing discomforts with each other's behaviour before. They had tended to approach matters indirectly or suppress their disappointments because, as they both admitted later, they believed that it could all be sorted out later 'when they had time'. It is a situation in which many couples find themselves. It is rather like the modern-day version of 'and they got married and lived happily ever after'. We know these days that there is more to it than that, but still put on the rosy-coloured spectacles for later years, as if everyone can comfortably slip into some Darby and Joan situation. And, of course, even if one slides gently into being a Darby, the other may have no wish to be a Joan!

The distressing truth is that the divorce rate is rising rapidly among couples in their Second Half. Being together for 20 years these days is no guarantee of being together for the next 20. And, as for divorces at any age, around 80% of the time it is initiated by the women, with their partners often complaining, 'I never saw it coming'.

It is just as I was always taught in counselling: there is always a risk attached wherever one party is approaching or moving through a major transition. Relationships can be a wonderful and solid support at those times, but they are also likely to be at their most fragile.

In the case of Gary and Anne they continued to try to deal with the situation indirectly. Anne picked faults with Gary in front of her friend and generally tried to make their outings together as unpleasant as possible for him in the hope that he would decide, of his own volition, to stop joining them. Unfortunately it had the opposite to her desired effect. Gary began to lose confidence in himself because of her jibes, sought even less external companionship without her, yet still failed to make the connection between her bad temper and his accompanying of her whenever she went out. If anything, he became more needy, yearning for validation and approval.

It eventually became so painful that it was their daughter, who had weathered a divorce herself, who flagged up warning signs to her mother and suggested they go to counselling. They both continued to put it off for several months, worried that by going to counselling after so many years of marriage they might, in Gary's words, 'be tempting Fate' or in Anne's, 'opening up a Pandora's box' that might mean the whole relationship would be blown sky high.

This is, of course, a very common concern, but just as fallacious as when people say they put off going to the doctor in case it's something serious.

Their happy ending (or, rather, happy continuation) is that they both became reluctant converts to the process. They were introduced to one of my favourite books, *I never knew I had a choice* by Gerald Corey and Mari-anne Schneider Corey, and found that they gained new communication tools and a safe environment in which to practise them. Far from being the hurtful or inflammatory experience they had feared, they found themselves intensely relieved that they could be guided through thorny areas of potential conflict without dodging the issues or ending up in an argument. And the sorts of conversations they were able to have around a broader range of relationship issues were enhanced too, and actually became a pleasure and an intellectual and emotional stimulation to them as opposed to an anxiety.

> 'I'm not sure they were even new tools. Just ones we used to know when we first got together, but which had ended up rusty,' Anne reflected. 'And somewhere along the line, pride or maybe fear got in the way of us using them together.'

Those with dual incomes often seem to initiate and manage such a dialogue somewhat more easily than the couples in which the male was the major or only breadwinner. It is not invariably the case though, and is again an area for conscious consideration.

Mike and Alison had been married for eight years when Mike was offered voluntary redundancy, aged 59. It was the second marriage for both of them. They were comfortably off, and Mike found himself feeling rather relieved that the responsibility for taking the decision about when to leave had been taken out of his hands. He was keen to spend more time on a small online business that he had started, and started making plans for them to move full-time to their second home in Devon. It was only when he asked Alison whether she had a preference for the estate agent they should use to sell their London property that they realised quite how far apart their expectations were:

> We'd always talked in general terms about being able to give up the stresses of the city and our jobs and move out to the country full-time, instead of just at weekends and holidays. I guess I always assumed that I was the one who was dragging my feet, and that Alison would be only too pleased to drop everything as soon as I gave the okay.

His wife, who is 13 years younger than Mike, felt side-swiped by the process:

I suppose in some ways I *had* been going along with the dream that once Mike gave up his city job we'd both change gears and probably do a sea change. It's just that when it came down to it I realized I wasn't ready. I've hardly been in my new role for a year and if I can pull this off successfully I'm literally going to move into the big time. I don't want to give it all away right at this point. I'm worried that if I do I'll end up resentful and blaming Mike. Unfortunately, it means we will pretty much have to go back to the drawing board to work out what this is going to mean.

Sometimes what looks like the perfect script turns out to need some extensive editing. Mike and Alison are still in the process of negotiating how their next few years are going to play out. In their case they wish they had talked earlier about some of the real practicalities involved in a major career shift, but consider themselves resilient enough to work their way through the considerations:

'Every situation is dynamic. Things often change incrementally, almost imperceptibly. It's quite understandable that what we said when we first got together, when we were both at different stages in our lives and careers, would be open to change. We kind of forgot to keep checking that, though' was Mike's view. 'But we are exploring what that means, and I'm sure we can come up with some solutions that work out well for both of us and are based on a shared reality and love for each other.'

The subject of friends should also form part of the 'training' if one is to feel like a winner in the Second Half. It is also one where many men, in particular, run into difficulties. Many A-type professionals tell me quite openly that their wives organise all their social events and that the friends they have are really more her friends than theirs. The couples with whom they go on skiing weekends are not always likely to be available for a round of golf, lunch or coffee midweek, especially if it's just with him; and, besides, the men say they often end up finding the only thing they have in common is the fact that their wives share a friendship. When pressed they will often make the comment that they simply do not have time to make friends 'of their own', nor keep up with older friends from school days or university. Work colleagues are very often described as friends, although in reality there is often little or no contact outside the work environment.

It can be a sad awakening then that, once off the traditional career ladder, the work colleagues drift out of contact and have little time or inclination to connect. Old school friends often have an annoying habit of moving away or overseas, so may become merely 'virtual' friends on email and no use for regular, 'Hey, let's meet up' type companionship. What happens to friendship and intimate, meaningful communication at this point? It can be particularly poignant that, just when one is experiencing a pull towards community and Generativity, the support and joy of close personal friendship can seem further away than ever.

Friendship is an aspect of energy sources which, in my consulting, I recommend should always be on the agenda at all points in one's personal and professional training. It shouldn't be a subject which comes to light only in the Emergency Surgery of the final days of one's later-career. Friendship, like romantic love, cannot occur to order. It cannot be bought, and it cannot be relied upon to turn up just when you want it. It needs to be cultivated and nurtured.

I firmly believe that people who are avid joiners or leaders of societies, alumni groups, sports clubs or professional or community associations are making as astute an investment as in stocks and shares. And those who maintain writing, calling and seeing friends as a priority, however manic their workload, are creating their own karma. It should not be hard to see that the caring and conscious cultivation of friendships and intimate contact forms one of the best bases for all the rest of the aspects on the wheel: physical wellbeing, fulfilling and meaning achievement, fun and leisure and the continuing developing of self and/or spirituality.

One of the most fascinating and inspirational examples of friendship in the Second Half that I have come across is one I see as demonstrating the rich possibilities of generative male friendship and personal growth. The story of it, I believe, is exceptionally worth telling, as I am sure there must be an enormous number of individuals and small networks of friends who would leap at the chance to do some of the things these men have done.

The group, based in Melbourne, Australia, calls itself Men Ageing Badly, a wordplay on the popular British comedy series 'Men Behaving Badly'. They are men who have known each other for a couple of decades or more and come from a cross-section of senior roles: politics, law, policy-making, commerce and architecture. The group itself started out around 10 years ago, when they were all in their early to late 50s, as a series of one-to-one lunches. Gradually, when they began sharing notes, they realised that their most compelling conversations were touching on the sort of topics that had pretty much been taboo to them before, centring around real-life fears, dreams and uncertainties. They were intrigued as to why this change seemed to be happening, and even more intrigued to hear further details about what each one of them was thinking.

They began arranging casual lunchtimes together, about once a month and each time with a different theme to discuss. These covered subjects like sex, health, relationships, career, beliefs and family. After a couple of them it was decided these would be best if facilitated by members in turn, not to make the sessions more formal but so as to avoid a natural tendency to move away from more 'difficult' issues once the conversation started to penetrate into really deep and sensitive areas. As Neil Watson, one of the founders of the group, explained, it was unanimously agreed they had more to gain and enjoy by not 'letting themselves off the hook'.

The sessions were taped by mutual consent of the group. Each one of them found the conversations exhilarating, comparing them to the intellectual and emotional rush of the type of exchanges they used to enjoy when at university. According to Neil, they became aware that they had lost the same depth and openness with other men over the years since they were students, commenting that whilst they might have discussed sexual concerns and career vulnerabilities with their wives and partners, it would have happened rarely, if ever, with other male friends or family.

In Neil's view it seemed that the timing was right for all sorts of reasons, and that it demonstrates Generativity in practice:

> Somehow, in our 40s, it would have been difficult to be so open. There was too much of a sense of competition and worry about losing face then. With some of the issues we've ended up discussing, particularly around sex and around our work, we would have been too concerned about 'if it got out'. I think we are all more secure in our own skins these days and, more importantly, what has been fascinating for all of us is that we all seem to be at a stage in our lives when we have a real thirst for a greater degree of intimacy and connection. It's at a far deeper level than we would have given our permission for before.
>
> Some people have asked whether it all came together because we were at some crisis points in our lives. But I don't think that's it. I think we simply found each other at a time when we were all looking for a *framework* for psychological support, not just a transactional occasional connection.

The generative approach became apparent early on too in their shared interest in their role as fathers. After decades of varying degrees of anxiety about whether they had given sufficient time, and indeed love, to their children the group came up with a radical suggestion:

> We decided to ask them! As simple as that. And it was interesting, because our main anxieties seemed to centre on what our sons thought of us. Probably because each of us found we harboured some unresolved issues around our own fathers, and felt the sadness of so many things left unsaid and unexplained. And I think because, without exception, none of our own fathers were still alive at the time we felt the urgency to try to avoid that same situation occurring between our own generation and our sons.
>
> So we decided to set up a dinner and invited all our sons to come. Frankly, in the run up to it, there were some jitters. We were all wondering, what would they say? Would they embarrass me? How would I feel about hearing some home truths, especially in front of my friends? Not all of the father–son relationships had been plain sailing, and it would be fair to say that some were still rather troubled.
>
> The basic question we asked our sons was 'What was it like having a successful, busy father?' The feedback was extraordinary. They were so candid, so honest, so . . . loving, it was very moving. They were probably all far more forgiving and understanding to us about any shortcomings they might have felt in the relationship than we were to ourselves.
>
> And of course it was fascinating to hear those of them who already had kids of their own, voicing their concerns about exactly the same issues around work, family time and communicating with their own boys. It was quite humbling that they were so appreciative of the opportunity to share their feelings with us. The dynamics were like nothing any of us had come across before, I think. I wouldn't be at all surprised if a number of them have gone away and set up similar discussions among their own male peers. They said it had given them the courage to, which was an unexpected bonus. Without any doubt it has taken the relationship we each have, with each of our sons, to a different level of closeness and honesty.

I asked Neil whether it had been the same sort of experience when they invited their daughters:

> Strangely enough it wasn't. For some reason we seemed to be expecting our daughters to be gentler and more understanding of us than our sons. Yet the reaction at that dinner was far more mixed. One of us mentioned afterwards that maybe it was more noticeable because, as women, they seemed far more at ease and practiced at sharing their emotions in that sort of environment. It was nowhere near such unfamiliar territory to them as it seemed to us and our sons. Maybe they felt freer and more able to articulate the mixed emo-

tions? I don't know. But there was no doubt, in both cases, that we all felt intensely privileged and humbled by the experience.

I also questioned him as to whether he felt the focus of the group had changed at all over the 10 years it had been going:

> Without a doubt. It reflects the way our lives are developing and changing too. We've worked through the retirement type of transition, and the sexual and relationship issues that can accompany that. Now one of the big issues that is starting to come on our radar is health. One of our group has Parkinson's disease. He was probably the brightest, most active and charismatic of everyone, so accompanying him through it is a sobering experience. It's uncomfortable to confront, but I'm immensely grateful we have the chance to talk openly about how he feels about it, how we all feel about it, and the impact it has.
>
> And of course that means that death is becoming a topic too. Dying and the death of our parents, our siblings, our friends. At some point the death of our partners, and our own death. We aren't used to talking about that sort of thing in our society any more, certainly not the emotional side of it. And it is very, very hard to talk about. But it's about as real as you can get. I'm really glad this gives us the framework, the permission and the . . . safety to explore it.

Men Ageing Badly seems to have come together spontaneously, and evolved organically. I don't see anything wrong in giving circumstances a helping hand, though, if such a situation doesn't occur quite so fortuitously. In Neil's opinion, its development was spurred by a couple of movers and shakers who made a point of pushing the group just that little bit beyond their comfort zone each time. As men who all responded well to a challenge, they found that approach both stimulating and attractive.

One option to explore could be to float the concept among a group which gets together regularly. It may turn into a fascinating one-off or beget a series, possibly for a subset which self-selects. One group I know of ex-student politicians, who have been getting together a few times a year since the early 1980s, had what turned out to be one of their most memorable meetings when the first of their number to turn 50 set everyone some direct questions about how they felt about their lives to date, their choices and their attitudes to reaching the Second Half.

Another two individuals I met decided to form a Book Club which, instead of contemplating their reactions to works of fiction as would be the norm, decided to select books on life transitions, self-awareness, spiritual development in the broadest sense and even some biographies and auto-biographies of individuals with a distinctive stance on life in the Second Half. It continues to grow by invitation and word of mouth, with its members enjoying what they describe as the benefits of an 'existential MBA' over a glass of good wine.

Some societies are more used to structured discussion and mutual learning than others. In Sweden it is estimated that at any given time 25% of the adult population is engaged in at least one self-directed Study Circle. Simi-larly, faith-based groups which are accustomed to Bible or literature study seem to find it relatively easy to form spin-offs to look at major life issues or form mutual-support groups for those going through testing transitions and change.

Another interesting example I have come across are the Westhill Con-versations, set up by Michael Morgan and his wife in New South Wales and spreading to the UK. Whilst these are not aimed at any particular age group or gender, the themes they choose for their regular get-togethers have obvious appeal to those for whom Generativity is, or is becoming, important in their lives. As the group Men Ageing Badly realised, we so often lack stimulating, searching, rigorous discussions and 'debates' these days in our day-to-day lives. Conversations with the same old friends and partners can become very predictable. There is usually more stagnancy than challenge, yet a common undercurrent in the Second Half is a yearning to revisit and talk through issues of import and meaning.

At Westhill, between eight and twenty people tend to turn up each time, a mixture of regulars and occasional attendees, and divide themselves into groups of four to six for the conversation. At the end there is a plenary debrief session with individual and group feedback about what transpired. When I've been myself I have most enjoyed the sense that it is almost played like a sport. Unlike with normal friendship groups no-one ever has to worry about offending anyone else, or concern themselves with the social dynam-ics or internal politics of the group.

It is like the most refreshing form of intellectual 'fencing'. Recent con-versation starters at Westhill have ranged from 'How to change the world: Some hints from Karl Marx and Che Guevara', through 'Complexity, despair and hope: on being a citizen of the world' to 'Somersaults and Dreams – perspectives on the year'.

So, whilst love and friendship cannot appear to order, the opportunities are many and various, and open to initiative, for nurturing intimacy and close interpersonal connections as a necessary part of one's own growth.

Fun and leisure

One of the strangest distortions concerning the Second Half, particularly that period beyond working 'for a living', is that life should then somehow turn into a holiday every day. It is a double-edged sword. Admittedly it is better than the bleak pre-20th century view that later life would be a steady sad decline into ill-health and poignant memories of happier times. Yet positioning the ideal Second Half as unrelenting beer and skittles actually sets up a host of counterproductive pressures and unrealistic expectations. For one thing, a diet consisting of only champagne and caviar is not just unhealthy but also destined to become boring after a time too.

Every year hundreds and thousands of new retirees fall for this misrepresentation. They go travelling, they buy a boat, they play golf every other day, they sunbathe by the pool and they take themselves out for the lunches and dinners they never had time for whilst working full-on. Of course there is nothing wrong in that. Far from it. It is a wonderful way to destress, reward oneself and generally have a good time getting the endorphins going.

When someone is at a point of a radical transition in later-career, a prolonged period of fun and leisure can be of great assistance in making the change easier and providing an antidote to grief. The caveat here is that it is a honeymoon period, just like in any new relationship or activity.

Generally it lasts between 18 months and two-and-a-half years. That is somewhat longer than the usual honeymoon period for a job, before one recognises that many of the same problems exist wherever one goes and that no organisation is perfect. One person I know comments ruefully, 'Funny. My problems always seem to turn up just where I do.'

Unless mentally prepared for it, once the novelty has worn off, the buzz of free time and no responsibilities can soon turn into *too much* time and *too lacking* in responsibilities. At some point a sense of anti-climax and boredom is likely to kick in, causing a misplaced sense of guilt for suddenly not enjoying it all 'as much as one should'. Unless counter-balanced by some meaningful activity and sense of self, the 'holiday' can turn into a mood-depressing 'Is that all there is?'

Ex-colleagues have a special knack of insensitivity around this in many cases. Their teasing, or their genuine assumption, that a life of leisure is paradise can become very wearing. It can feel far too much pressure to live up to, like the myth that everyone else is having fantastic fun over Christmas or on vacation when the real truth is that they are the most stress-producing times of the year as everyone is trying to live up to the ideal of 'the perfect holidays'.

It's not that there have to be hard and fast dates set for how long this honeymoon period is likely to last. The important thing is to maintain the awareness that at some point the gilt is likely to wear off the gingerbread, and it could well start to feel as if a surfeit of undirected leisure is an energy depleter, not an energy source.

Don't worry if that happens. If you don't have anything to step into immediately, what you will have is the pleasure to look forward to of *exploring* and *planning* what that might turn out to be. It's all a question of balancing the wheel and the energy sources – the really grown-up version of work–life balance.

At the other end of the spectrum there are some folk who seem to feel downright uncomfortable about accepting and enjoying some sort of break or later-career sabbatical. I've seen them fight against it and be over-eager to find something (anything!) to replace what they saw as the benefits of work. It is a pity for them, and probably an even greater pity for their partners and families that they are denying themselves a highly valid source of re-energisation.

The best advice I find is to keep in mind some future date to either start some meaningful work-like activities, or at least a date to allow yourself to start thinking about them. But in the meantime go ahead and revel in the long break you've probably denied yourself for years.

Again, the greater the awareness one has that it *is* a honeymoon period, the greater the ability one has to enjoy and appreciate it for what it is.

Fun and leisure doesn't have to be an ON/OFF button with work either. The concepts are not polar opposites. They can integrate. The trend among generation X and Y is towards regular mini-sabbaticals/long breaks interspersed throughout their careers. It seems an exceptionally sensible method to pace themselves for what they know will be an Extended Career, and to give themselves a decent time to recharge batteries instead of snatching a handful of short breaks which do not allow for the same degree of reflection and re-energisation.

I'm seeing a growing number of Second Halfers prioritising such breaks as an integral part of their later-career too. In comparison with part-time work, project work offers greatest scope. Charles Handy and Alistair Mant, both renowned authors and speakers on management and leadership themes and both began this practice when approaching their 70s. At the start of the year they work out what interests them, what their leisure preferences are – then target or accept work options which allow them the time, flexibility and related travel to indulge that.

Purposeful activity/work

Although we may complain about the stresses and pressures of work, the purposeful activity it provides for us satisfies a number of our basic human needs. Researchers into the social implications of work note that there are five major such 'benefits' to working. During the course of our lives we get so attached to them that we cannot discard them without some emotional and psychological consequences. For most of us, we don't want to either, as purposeful activity and work are sources of fuel for us too.

That is one of the reasons I have preferred to coin the terms later-career and Extended Career, and generally avoid the word 'retirement'. For successful players during the First Half, keen to keep in a winning position, continuing some form of meaningful work and activity is imperative. It therefore deserves to be termed a *continuing* career, or an extended one, whether the work is part-time, full-time or project and whether it is highly paid, an average reward or purely voluntary.

It is important to understand what these benefits are, as the subsets of this one energy source, and how we can maintain and/or replace them through the remainder of our lives.

The first, and usually most obvious, is *financial remuneration*. As I've pointed out often already, many people count this as their sole focus of retirement preparation. In practical terms there is obviously a need to ensure that living expenses can still be paid, and that there is some degree of comfort to cater for emergencies.

However, very often people severely underestimate the psychological impact of loss of income. It is the status symbol effect, rather than the money itself. Coming to grips with the fact that there will be no more grandly increasing salary, and no hefty bonuses can be a blow to confidence. Subliminally, and of course quite wrongly, high-achievers may be seeing themselves in the equation: no pay rise + no bonus = loser.

And sometimes the hardest adjustment for high-performers is not going from salary to pension, but from a highly paid to a low or lower-paid role. In those instances it is also about another of the benefits, *status*, rather than the money itself. An international airline pilot who had taken early retirement told me how unexpectedly awkward his own transition had felt:

> I like the outdoors, I was never able to indulge my enjoyment of garden work in my old job, so I took on a franchise of mowing, pool cleaning and a bit of gardening. It has been great, as I can choose what I do, where and when I choose to do it, and I use any money I earn on absolute treats for myself. Lovely silly stuff. But what wasn't so great was the reaction I sensed from the neighbours. I could never quite work out whether they were horrified or sorry for me. I think they assumed I'd had some sort of financial meltdown and had to make ends meet by doing something terribly menial. Either that or I'd been sacked ignominiously and couldn't get anything more responsible! They seemed to have a real suburban chip on their shoulder that doing pools and gardens should have been beneath 'someone like me'.
>
> It went from being, 'Oooh, we've got a *pilot* living next door to us!' and being one of the interesting people on the block, to worrying that they thought I was going to default on my mortgage or start bringing car wrecks into the front yard. It's like they would have preferred it if I'd just stayed home and become a vegetable or something. Fortunately, as these things do, there must have been someone else who came and provided some greater scandal, and I'm accepted as a harmless curiosity now.
>
> And I'm still having fun doing what I'm doing. I've found my status in some of the other interests I've taken up. I'm being an Activist again, lobbying on climate change and the environment. Their sense of status is stuck in the jobs.

A further benefit of a work routine to remember is *time management*. The odd thing here is that women/spouses always intuit what this is going to mean and know that their partner is likely to be all at sea and rudderless without the framework that work provides. Men, on the other hand, usually fail to see it coming. Only entrepreneurs, used to running their own ship, seem to manage to develop a sort of inner clock-cum-scheduler which allows them to keep on track whatever they move on to do.

For those in other forms of employment, work gives our life structure and effectively manages our time. For many accustomed to putting in a 24/7 commitment, the loss of structure can be debilitating. Our work usually lets us know what we'll be doing come next Monday morning. In fact, it usually arranges it for us. It keeps our lives orderly, we are 'in the loop' and in the mainstream, connected to the company culture and colleagues. Without that structure it is easy to fritter away days at a time, then end up feeling guilty and ineffectual.

This is not just an issue confined to retirees or the newly redundant. Later-career is often a time for developing portfolio work and projects. So it is vital to confidence and performance to develop one's own routine and pace for these.

Linked to the benefits of family and friends is the *socialisation* aspect that work brings. In our work environments we are in close contact, even 'virtually', with a variety of other people. We interact with them, we develop relationships, learn to co-operate at higher and higher levels, share information and negotiate. In this case it's not about forming friendships, but the fact that as complex creatures we thrive on the connections and interactions provided by a work situation and can feel stagnant, lonely and diminished without it.

It is something that people setting up their own businesses, or working in virtual environments are warned about. When I set up my first company, Re-Inventors, several years ago, and latterly when I have been writing and spending days on my own with minimal external contact, I have really felt the pain of it. It's not just the gregarious sorts who miss it either. The stimulation created through socialisation is a definite source of energy for all.

The fifth need which work answers is *purpose*. The most successful firms create a culture which engenders a sense of purpose in all their workers, whether they make commodities like widgets or cars or such useful things to humanity as making humidified cribs for premature babies.

Whatever stage we are at in our career, our life is given implicit meaning and validity through our work by assisting others in some way, by servicing their needs. We all have a need to be needed. Our work gives us a 'cause', a sense of internal status and meaning as opposed to the external status of title, power or salary. In a period of our lives, in later-career, when Generativity becomes important to us, the urge to feel useful and have a purpose is particularly pronounced.

Continuous learning

This is an energy source closely linked to purposeful activity and work. All research that I know concurs that workers who are pro-active in keeping themselves abreast of new learning are those who suffer least from the plateau syndrome. And if they find themselves boxed in, or plateaued, they are more likely to have the confidence to seek alternatives directly connected with their new learnings.

Similarly, all employers I know admit that the first people in later-career whom they target for redundancy, or whom they *consciously* restrict to a final plateau, are those who do not demonstrate a commitment to continuous learning and personal development. The paradox of this is, as we have seen, that very few organisations bother to devote their own budget to active training of later-career workers so their judgement concerning what constitutes a 'continuous learner' may not necessarily be the most accurate.

The findings from the Harvard studies by George Vaillant also demonstrate the benefits of ongoing learning. It is perfectly easy to 'teach old dogs new tricks' – and they are all the happier and healthier for it. Keeping one's mind active through challenging mental pursuits and the uptake of stimulating new material is now proven to keep the brain function sharp and significantly delay the process of mental degeneration, and possibly even ward off Alzheimer's.

On the above evidence, it is clearly highly valuable to cultivate a proactive attitude towards learning in later-career and beyond. It is also worthwhile to test your own assumptions about your involvement with learning and personal development. It is quite common for people with graduate and postgraduate qualifications to take it for granted that they are learners by nature. However, closer inspection often reveals that it may have been over 30 years since they attended any formal educational activities – and that even informal educational opportunities have been very rare in that same period too.

In Chapter 5 the point emerged that in order to pursue one's later-career intentions and achieve Significance there may be a need to augment one's current skills and behaviours with new ones. At this point in one's life identification of those new requirements should be stemming from personal choice. The way to check this out is whether the learning you feel drawn to, or consider you need to undertake, feels attractive and compelling. It may well feel slightly daunting. There should possibly even be a slight sense of trepidation within the excitement if it is genuinely stimulating and taking one on the road to new Significance.

And the scope of learning in later-career can extend from hard skills like book-keeping and desktop publishing to self-awareness development through meditation, retreats or counselling. One of the most inspiring examples I've come across recently of truly self-empowering, energy-generating personal development was the story of the 88-year-old male ballet dancer in the UK.

John Lowe, from Cambridgeshire, took up ballet at the age of 79. In January 2008, at 88 years old, he performed on stage for the first time at The Maltings, in Prokofiev's 'The Stone Flower'. In a neat reversal of influencing roles, he says he took it up because he saw how much his daughter, a professional dancer herself, enjoyed it. Showing a total ease with himself and his passion, John was quoted on the BBC news saying, 'It's a wonderful thing to do. I don't know why more men don't do it.'

Many learning opportunities are absolutely free. They may be found in learning-by-doing, increased reading and studying, or they may be provided free by educational institutions. Alternatively they may be quite costly, so test also your attitudes to *paying* for continuous learning. When one is out of the habit of paying for something like study (and was perhaps brought up in an era of full student grants too) it can feel like a challenge to one's principles to be expected to pay for development opportunities. There may also be a sense of frustration and unfairness if one believes it is the employer's duty to pay – yet one which is not forthcoming. Additionally later-career, especially later-career redundancy, can be a time of *over*-prudence financially. Check that it is not being exacerbated by a punishing self-denial, either in the form of 'I'm not worthy of that sort of expense' or 'I don't need that sort of expensive training'.

Those potentially self-limiting beliefs are clearly linked with the concept of 'enough' too. It is rather sad, if not slightly pathetic, to hear extremely well off, successful executives complain that they are not prepared to spend 'that sort of money!' on their own self- and spiritual development yet have no qualms about buying cases of wine, financing house extensions or flying out for a week of winter sun. The saying, 'Show me your cheque book and I'll tell you who you are' is absolutely true.

Self and spirituality

For my own part I see self and spirituality as two sides of the same coin and intrinsically linked with the concept of Generativity. They are at the centre of the wheel, the axle point. If those are balanced, the wheel can turn easily. If they are out of whack, whatever else you do with the other sectors the trajectory will always be bumpy and wobbly.

Referring to one's spirituality I do not necessarily mean one's religion, although we can certainly express our spirituality through religion. For example, I consider myself a spiritual person, and am happy to say 'I speak Christian'. By that I mean that I am familiar and comfortable with the beliefs and vocabulary of Christianity, as I was brought up in them, and it is a beautiful shared language that I learned which can communicate spiritual themes precisely and articulately.

But, like many others, I feel that my spirituality transcends organised religion and these days has more to do with trying to understand and honour the connectedness of all things, living creatures and pure matter, the tangible and the intangible. Indeed, one definition I have come across defines spirituality as the personal, subjective element of religion.

It is the search for the metaphysical – that which is greater than the physical dimensions which we can see. Literally, spirituality is the search and respect for the spirit which propels and energises all things. To be truly immersed in it is to desire to combine with, and offer love and help to, all people, all creatures, our planet and the universe beyond it, both now and for the future good. Which takes us back to Generativity.

For some, the Second Half is a time when faith blossoms or deepens, or when it is encountered and accepted for the first time. It is rare that those who find or increase their spirituality in this half become zealots and persecutors of others who do not share their belief, unlike the tendency in the First Half. Yet the energy it generates within them often shines far more brilliantly, and attracts more interest simply through the appeal of its warmth and ability to light the way for others.

Robin Squire, previously British Conservative Member of Parliament for a number of years, now in his 60s used to attend Church intermittently but believes he has found a deeper connection with spirituality beyond that now – a very personal connectivity with 'all that'. He says that he tried to live his mission in politics as loving and helping others, but that a new sense of self at his stage in life has lifted the barrier of fear that so many of us suffer from when actually trying to put this into practice.

The starting point for true spirituality is the self. In Robin's words, 'We all develop from within, not without'. Our self is a microcosm of the world and the universe. If we are to consider ourselves spiritual in any way, and eager for greater enlightenment on the metaphysical, we must start at home – knowing, loving and accepting ourselves first.

Even those who may feel uncomfortable with the concept of spirituality, and see themselves as purely rational, physical beings tend still to be drawn to the self as they move into the Second Half. This is not as self-absorption, but as self-awareness, self-acceptance and self-actualisation.

As we have explored throughout these chapters, often the most difficult thing to do in our lives has been to get to know ourselves and to follow our own locus of control. In our early career choices we have innocently bought in to others' agendas. Further along we have probably somewhere abdicated our responsibility for self-direction to become part of a comfortable crowd, and we have suppressed our true desires and passions until we may not even recall what they once were.

In the Second Half we have the opportunity to take back that control and care for the self again. By this age we are often parents, caring diligently for a child but perhaps still shying away from caring for our self.

Caring, nurturing and knowing our self does not mean selfishness and pandering to ego. It means tending a fine specimen, at a point where ego is no longer needed for growth so that in turn it is best equipped to tend others through Generativity.

In the Second Half we are at our peak, the sum of all experiences and learnings, all triumphs and disappointments. With each day passing we become more unique, more exceptional.

To rework a phrase from Tolstoy, 'All youths resemble one another. Each older person is unique in their own distinctive way.'

***

DEVELOPING THE GAMEPLAN:
Remaining a winner throughout

Questions & activities to help you remain at the top of, and even improve on, your game for the rest of the Second Half

1. Energy sources – are you properly plugged in?

How much time and focus do you give to each of the energy sources to allow you to maintain and improve your performance?

In the circle below, draw in how much time/focus you **currently** give:

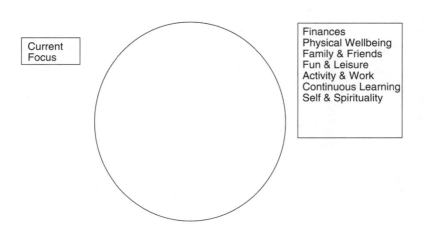

Current Focus

Finances
Physical Wellbeing
Family & Friends
Fun & Leisure
Activity & Work
Continuous Learning
Self & Spirituality

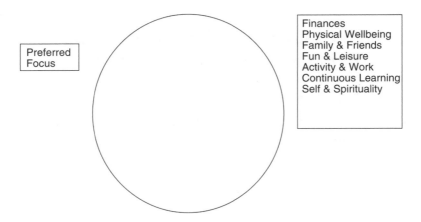

In the circle above, draw in how much time you would **prefer** to give to each.

2. Your energy sources SWOT analysis

Look at your potential energy sources more closely.

For each of the topics ask yourself the following questions:

What do I do well here?
What could I do better?
What would I most like to achieve/get out of this aspect of life?

Find time to ask your partner, a friend and/or close family member how they see what you do well and what you could do better in each category.

Ask them what they would most wish for you under each or any of the headings.

Looking at the categories are there any things you know you ought to tell yourself, or advice you should give yourself – but very rarely do?

What are the three most important priorities for me in order to develop my Preferred Focus?

What major steps will I commit to make in the next week? And what support and/or monitoring will I seek from other quarters to ensure I keep on track?

References

Adler, Claire (2006) 'Mix and Match', (2006) The Guardian, November 4.

Anderson, R. (1999) *Mid-course Correction: Towards a Sustainable Enterprise: The Interface Model*. Peregrinzilla Press, February.

APG+DWP (2006) Report by Age Partnership Group and Department for Work & Pensions.

AXA (2007) AXA Retirement Scope 2007: Executive Summary.

Beck, D. and Cowan, C. (2005) *Spiral Dynamics: Mastering values, leadership and change*. John Wiley & Sons, June.

Bridges, W. (2001) *The Way of Transition: Embracing life's most difficult moments*. Da Capo Press, February.

Broad, W.J. (2008) 'Smart machines ready to assume many NASA duties', *New York Times*, 10 January.

Buford, B. (1997) *Halftime: Changing your gameplan from Success to Significance*. Zondervan Publishing House, April.

Bunyan, J. (1996) *The Pilgrim's Progress* (Wordsworth Classics of World Literature). Wordsworth Editions Ltd, November.

Chopra, D. (1993) *Ageless Body, Timeless Mind*. Harmony Books.

Cohen, G.D. (2001) *The Creative Age: Awakening human potential in the second half of life*. Harper Paperbacks, January.

Cohen, G.D. (2005) *The Mature Mind*. Basic Books, December.

Collins, J. (2001) *Good to Great: Why some companies make the leap . . . and others don't*. Collins, October.

Corey, G. and Schneider Corey, M. (2005) *I Never Knew I Had a Choice*. Wadsworth Publishing, 8th edition, March.

Dychtwald, K. (2000) *Age Power: How the 21st century will be ruled by the new old*. Tarcher, September.

Dychtwald, K. and Flower, J. (1990) *The Age Wave: How the most important trend of our time can change your future*. Bantam, January.

Erikson, E. (1993) *Childhood and Society*. WW Norton and Company, August.

Euridyce Report (2002). 'The Teaching Profession in Europe: Profile, Trends and Concerns', www.Euridyce.org.

Forte, C. and Hansvick, C. (1999) A study of workers over and under age 50, *Journal of Employment Counselling* **36**(1).

Freeman, G. (2008) *The Business Olympian*. New Holland, July.

Friedan, B. (2006) *The Fountain of Age*. Simon and Schuster, August.

Gilligan, C. (1993) *In a Different Voice: Psychological theory and women's development*. Harvard University Press, July.

Gould, R. (1979) *Transformations: Growth and change in adult life*. Simon and Schuster, 1st Touchstone edition, August.

Hawken, P. (1994) *The Ecology of Commerce*. Collins, June.

Highland Partners (2004) Survey: 'The Ageing Workforce, an Executive Perspective'.

HSBC (2006) 'The Future of Retirement: What businesses want'.

Joseph, J. (1997) *Warning – When I am an Old Woman I shall Wear Purple*. Souvenir Press Ltd, November.

Kaeuper, R.W. (2005) *William Marshal, Lancelot, and the Issue of Chivalric Identity*. Essays in Medieval Studies 22, West Virginia University Press.

Kofman, F. (2006) *Conscious Business: Creating value through values*. Sounds True, September.

Kotre, J. (1984) *Outliving the Self: Generativity and the interpretation of lives*. The John Hopkins University Press, November.

Levinson, D. (1986) *The Seasons of a Man's Life*. Ballantine Books, May.

McAdams, D.P. (2001) 'Generativity, the new definition of success', *Spirituality & Health*, Fall.

Ministerial Advisory Committee on Ageing (2007) Report by Ministerial Advisory Committee on Ageing, NSW, March.

O'Kelly, E. (2007) *Chasing Daylight – How my forthcoming death transformed my life*. McGraw-Hill, September.

OECD (2006) 'Report on Working'.

Petre, D. (2005) *Father Time*. Jane Curry Publishing, August.

Sheehy, G. (1996) *New Passages: Mapping your life across time*. Harpercollins Publishers, May.

Sheehy, G. (1999) *Understanding Men's Passages: Discovering the new map of men's lives*. Ballantine Books, May.

Singer, P. (1995) *How are we to live?: Ethics in an age of self-interest*. Prometheus Books.

Smith, F. (2007) 'Careers: the key is the care factor', *Boss Magazine, The Australian Financial Review*, 11 September.

University of Michigan (2007) 'Older Workers Stress Less, U-M Study Suggests', University of Michigan, News Services, 19 November.

Vaillant, G.E. (2003) *Aging Well: Surprising signposts to a happier life*. Little, Brown and Company, January.

Watts, T. (2007) 'Harnessing the skills of older workers', *Mature Times*, 14 November (www.maturetimes.co.uk).

Whitehall II (2004), Whitehall II Study, UCL, September.

Wilber, K. (2000) *Integral Psychology: Consciousness, spirit, psychology, therapy*. Shambhala, May.

Williams, J.P.R. (2006) *JPR: Given the breaks – my life in rugby*. Hodder and Stoughton Ltd, October.

www.ceoforum.com.au (2008) 'Creating the sustainable corporation: IAG's Mike Hawker', April 1.

www.maturetimes.co.uk (2008) 'New Year – new divorce for the over-50s', *Editorial*, www.maturetimes.co.uk, 4 January.

Index

Index compiled by Terry Halliday